PROFESSIONAL ETHICS IN EDUCATION SERIES

Kenneth A. Strike, Editor

The Ethics of School Administration
*Kenneth A. Strike, Emil J. Haller
and Jonas F. Soltis*

Classroom Life as Civic Education:
Individual Achievement and Student Cooperation in Schools
David C. Bricker

. . . by doing the acts that we do in our transactions with other men we become just or unjust, and by doing the acts that we do in the presence of danger, and being habituated to feel fear or confidence, we become brave or cowardly. The same is true of appetites and feelings of anger; some men become temperate and good-tempered, others self-indulgent and irascible, by behaving in one way or the other in the appropriate circumstances. Thus, in one word, states of character arise out of like activities. This is why the activities we exhibit must be of a certain kind; it is because the states of character correspond to the differences between these. It makes no small difference, then, whether we form habits of one kind or of another from our very youth; it makes a very great difference, or rather *all* the difference.

ARISTOTLE
Nicomachean Ethics, 1103b 14–26

CLASSROOM LIFE
AS
CIVIC EDUCATION

Individual Achievement
and
Student Cooperation in Schools

DAVID C. BRICKER

Teachers College, Columbia University
New York and London

Published by Teachers College Press, 1234 Amsterdam Avenue,
New York, NY 10027

Copyright © 1989 by Teachers College, Columbia University

Library of Congress Cataloging-in-Publication Data

Bricker, David C.
    Classroom life as civic education : individual achievement and
student cooperation in schools / David C. Bricker.
        p.   cm. — (Professional ethics in education series.
    Bibliography: p. 115
    Includes index.
    ISBN 0-8077-2959-0
    1. Civics—Study and teaching.   2. Political socialization—United
States.   3. Liberalism—United States.   4. Community.   5. Social
ethics.   I. Title.   II. Series.
LB1584.B67   1989
372.83'2044—dc20   89-31615
                                                                    CIP

ISBN 0-8077-2959-0

Manufactured in the United States of America
94 93 92 91 90 89   1 2 3 4 5 6 7

For
Jeffrey David
and
Jonathan Philip

Contents

Series Foreword

This is the second book in the Teachers College Press series, Professional Ethics in Education, which is devoted to the examination of ethical issues in all educational settings. The books that will be published in this series divide into three distinct groups.

The first group is intended to teach some central concepts of professional ethics to practitioners. These volumes will be built around case studies and will focus on helping practitioners to acquire or refine some of the concepts that are crucial in reflecting on ethical issues. The books will be brief and practically oriented. The first volume in the series, *The Ethics of School Administration*, was part of this group. The model for these books was *The Ethics of Teaching* by Kenneth Strike and Jonas Soltis, part of the Teachers College Press Thinking About Education Series, edited by Jonas Soltis.

The second group of titles will focus on pedagogical and curricular issues related to professional ethics. Intended to help in thinking through an approach to teaching about professional ethics, contributions in this group will pay special attention to the needs of those who are not formally trained in ethics as they strive to work out successful teaching strategies. Since it is our belief that the study of professional ethics should be diffused throughout the curriculum, we feel that books in this part of the series should be of value to all who are involved in the training of educational practitioners.

The third group of books will deal with issues of professional ethics in a rigorous and scholarly way. These volumes will be topical, treating current controversial issues in order to advance our knowledge and understanding of specific problems. They should be of interest to both scholars and practitioners who want the opportunity to think through a particular issue thoroughly.

David Bricker's book, *Classroom Life as Civic Education: Individual Achievement and Student Cooperation in Schools*, is the first book in this group. It is an excellent treatment of the importance of cooperative learning, set in the context of a debate between a liberal and a communitarian view of ethics. It thus relates an important current debate in philosophy to a significant practical concern of educators.

All of the books in this series will aim at helping teachers and the educational profession to examine and reflect on the ethical issues and controversies that are a normal and routine part of educational practice. We believe that this is an especially important task as education seeks to mold itself more on the model of a self-governing profession. Our world is not one in which eternal verities or the moral sentiments of a cohesive community can easily govern conduct in public institutions. Educators who wish to be responsible for the practice of education must therefore be equipped to take individual responsibility for thinking through defensible positions on difficult ethical questions. We hope this series will assist them in the endeavor.

KENNETH A. STRIKE
CORNELL UNIVERSITY

Foreword

I received my copy of David Bricker's manuscript, *Classroom Life as Civic Education*, in 1988, a few days prior to the first presidential debate between George Bush and Michael Dukakis. Perhaps then it was more likely that I would listen to the candidates with questions in the forefront of my mind about citizenship and how citizens are formed, and that I would react to the debate as an educator concerned about how our politics forms people.

Two things struck me. The first was the extent to which Americans seem to have lost sight of the fact that institutions form character. We treat our politics, our constitution, as though they were merely ways of making decisions. We have forgotten the lessons of Plato and Aristotle, that a society's constitution, its politics, its ways of conducting its collective business, and the forms that human associations take, are also—perhaps even primarily—ways of creating people and should be judged by the kinds of people they create. It is unfortunate that the character of modern political campaigns does much to confirm Plato's criticisms of democracy. His critique was an educational one. He believed that different forms of government not only reflect, but form, different kinds of character. Democracy was objected to by Plato because, he believed, it harms people; it makes them worse. Democracy affirms their appetites and passions, whatever their real worth, and undercuts the rule of reason in their lives.

Those who favor democratic institutions have also believed that democracy forms character. They have claimed that democracy makes people more competent, and that free people who must choose for themselves have an incentive to be competent. It is the slave, not the free person, who has no reason to develop the intellect. Likewise, participation in collective decision making is an educative process wherein people grow through sharing with one another their views on how their collective lives should be lived. Of course, those who have seen this potential in democratic life have also not missed the potential for demagoguery and irrationality in the political affairs of a democratic society. Such politics is best contained if we have already succeeded in producing individuals who refuse to respond to it and who demand instead reasoned argument about public affairs. Schools have been seen as the instruments to create such people. They are supposed to demonstrate the falsity of Plato's theory and to realize the possibilities inherent in discourse among free people.

It is common for pundits to object to contemporary politics by claiming that it is irrational. They believe we should elect our candidates by a rational appraisal of their views. Instead, candidates are sold to us as though they were deodorant or bars of soap. But the point of this objection is always about how our society makes its political decisions. It does not attend to how the form of communication reflects something about the character of modern Americans and how it reinforces and further develops this character. If we are sold candidates as though they were bars of soap, it must be that this is because we respond more readily to images and appeals to our appetites and passions than we do to political reason. One must wonder if the preponderance of selling over arguing in our lives helps make us this way. Certainly there is much in the modern political campaign that can be used to make a case for Plato. At the very least our politics suggests that there is much educational work to be done if Plato is to be shown to be wrong.

The second thing that impressed me about the presidential debate was that in some very important ways the conservative candidate, Mr. Bush, often struck a more liberal pose than his opponent. If this comment seems surprising or unintelligible, that may be because we have come to use the word 'liberal' in ways that disassociate it significantly from its roots. (After all, it now seems possible, without irony, to describe Mr. Gorbachev as a liberal in contrast to his orthodox Marxist-Leninist opponents who are, allegedly, conservatives.) The heart of liberalism is an emphasis on individual freedom. It is most accurate to see the United States as having two liberal parties: one which holds the view that government is the basic threat to personal liberty, and which seeks to constrain its power. The other holds that government power can be used as a tool to create and to fairly distribute the material basis of meaningful individual freedom, and serve as a check on the erosion of liberty that can result from the excesses of private power. What these views have in common is the sense of people as moral individuals with a right to pursue their own goods in their own way and of the government as an enforcer of the rules of fair competition. Mr. Bush may reject this liberal agenda with respect to what are sometimes called the "social issues." For instance, his views on abortion and school prayer are not liberal. But the liberal strain in his thought asserts itself forcefully in the rejection of governmental interference in other affairs of the family and in his vision of the economic role of government. Here we stand as individuals or as individual families with the right to our own lives and the need to pursue them in the marketplace. Our fate is ours to make and to undergo.

In contrast, Mr. Dukakis often emphasized the values of community. For him, prosperity and progress are good only when we all are brought along. That we tolerate homelessness and poverty is not simply undesirable because some right to economic fairness is violated. We are not exhorted to fight poverty because we owe some duty to the poor. Instead, it seems as though the toleration of poverty and homelessness are shameful because they offend against the values of community.

I am reminded of the comments of a tour guide whom I encountered last year in Zurich. She took pride in pointing out the facilities that Switzerland had constructed for the indigent aged. She noted the costs of such social programs and a high tax rate, but she found the fact that the Swiss took care of their own to be a source of satisfaction. She contrasted Swiss behavior with how Americans treat their fellow citizens. That Americans permit people to live and die on the streets seemed to be not so much a denial of welfare rights as a rupture of community. To her it was a source of shame, for the Swiss could not treat other Swiss in such a manner.

The appeal is not to some version of liberal economic rights. It is to the values of community in which people become human by achieving a collective identity, and in which the misfortune of one is felt as the misfortune of all. The essential appeal is not to liberal justice; it is to the goods of the community. We are not to encounter one another as moral agents to whom we owe various duties, but as friends, fellow countrymen, or fellow citizens. The virtues of community are not merely those of justice; they are friendship, generosity, or solidarity. These are what motivate members of a community to care for one another.

Like those of my Swiss tour guide, Mr. Dukakis's concerns about poverty seemed motivated more by communitarian sentiment than by a sense of liberal economic justice. Dukakis often talked about government as more a builder of community than as a regulator of competition between moral individuals, government as a builder of cooperation and consensus. For the governor, our economic and political life is to reflect collectively chosen consensual values, not the workings of the formed.

Bricker understands that the "constitution of schools" forms students' character. He also understands that in schools this process is often unintentional and inarticulate. Teachers do not see themselves as teaching political concepts, forms of discourse, or models of association in how they structure or talk about their students' work. Teachers' behavior is thus a part of the hidden curriculum. Moreover, most Americans now seem to lack the concepts required to discuss these issues in an articulate way. It would not be immediately clear to them without detailed explanation what it would mean to say that a teacher's discourse is liberal. In recent years (seemingly along with Allan Bloom and the rest of the world) I have taken to asking my students what they have read. Often I will ask students if they have read Locke, Marx, or Mill. The results are notable. Few students have read any part of any of these authors. Curiously, more students seem to have read some Marx than have read Locke or Mill. If they are out of touch with these sources, how are they to identify their discourse as liberal? Yet often they do talk and think in liberal ways. Those students who do not read Locke or Mill can use arguments assuming that governments must rest on the consent of the governed or that the pursuit of truth requires free and open discussion. Thus, they think as liberals, but they are unaware of the sources of their thought. Their liberal flowers lack future roots. This lack reduces their capacity to identify and to make articulate the liberal form of their discourse, or to recognize its consequences in their lives and that there are alternatives to it. Their capacity to be critical of their own lives is much reduced.

My students are, of course, prospective teachers. There is little reason (other than their taking a course from me) to suppose that there will be anything in invisible hand. It is the responsibility of political leadership to help form such consensual values. His membership in the American Civil Liberties Union (ACLU) notwithstanding, Mr. Dukakis's vision of democracy often seemed more communitarian than liberal.

Why talk about last year's political campaign here? The election is now over and done with. I have two reasons. The first is that both of the themes I attached to the 1988 election are crucial to the argument of David Bricker's book. Second, I want to show that these concerns are not just the arcane concerns of political philosophers. They have a reality that is expressed in our most central political institutions, but it is a reality that is often invisible to us because we have lost touch with too much of our political heritage. We lack the concepts with which to see.

One essential assumption of this book is that there is a kind of reciprocal relation between our institutions and our characters and basic beliefs. Professor Bricker wants to show that teacher discourse and practice is often structured in a certain way, which he calls "liberal egalitarian." Bricker suggests that teachers emphasize individual work to the extent that they do because they are motivated to have each student maximize his or her potential, while at the same time they seek to minimize invidious comparisons resulting from differences in individual capacity. These are concerns that teachers could not have unless they were given to thinking like liberals. They assume such liberal notions as, we are the owners of our capacities and as moral individuals we are entitled to equal respect. At the same time teacher discourse and practice form a part of the hidden curriculum. Students learn a form of discourse and a way of associating with each other from how teachers structure their work and how they talk about it. Thus is character the education that will make them more aware of their roots. Therefore, much of the political socialization they will provide their students will be unintentional, inarticulate, and uncritical.

It is one of the virtues of David Bricker's book that he is able to identify the political structure of ordinary teacher practice and

discourse. He offers to teachers and other educational professionals the opportunity to understand and reflect on how their discourse and practice forms the character of their students in a way
that few are now able to do.

One of my concerns about David Bricker's book is that those
for whom it is intended may find it difficult, arcane, and "irrele-
vant." But such reactions are more telling about those who make
them and about the poverty of current views of teacher education
than they are about Bricker's work or the topics he deals with. It is
currently fashionable to insist that teaching either is or should be a
profession. Professionals, of course, are given a long and rigorous
training in the knowledge base in which professional practice is
said to be grounded. It is instructive to note what is included in the
list of topics that generally are thought to comprise this knowledge base for teaching. Subject matter is always mentioned. Cognitive psychology and educational measurement are frequently
included as well. It is rare to mention that teachers might study
ethics or political philosophy. Even when ethics is mentioned, it
seems that what is meant is that it would be a good thing if
teachers were taught some reasonably straightforward code of
conduct prescribing how they are to deal with their students,
other teachers, parents, and administrators. (And indeed, it would
be a good thing.) But it is almost never suggested that teachers
should be taught to understand the basic moral and political concepts that underlie society. This is not suggested, although fre-
quent lip service is given to the view that schools are supposed to
train citizens for a democratic society.

Perhaps our views of teacher education indicate that we have
become mere technocrats about teaching, so that it has become
difficult for us to imagine any study as a relevant part of the
training of a teacher that does not result in a technique for teaching. Here, 'technique' means 'technique for the efficient transmis-
sion of information.'

David Bricker's work should, however, provide good reason
to motivate teacher educators to a higher level of seriousness about
the importance of the study of ethics and political philosophy for
teachers. For Bricker shows that teachers do have incipient political philosophies and that these political philosophies govern their
practice. Teachers who lack any serious study of ethics or political

philosophy will be unable to formulate the grounds of their practice. Their political intuitions will remain inarticulate. So long as this is the case, those practices that are generated by teachers' political and moral intuitions will remain part of the hidden curriculum. Teachers will not be able to recognize these incipient political views as objects of choice and reflection, and, in any case, they will lack the resources required for sophisticated thought about them.

It thus seems to me to be both extraordinary and tragic that we do not, as a rule, seriously attempt to educate prospective teachers in the political and moral conceptions that govern our society. That we do not do so condemns teachers to an intolerable degree of inarticulateness and unreflectiveness about matters that govern their work and their professional practice.

Professor Bricker's book assumes that how teachers think is the source of how they behave. We should note an alternative: that teacher behavior is dictated by structural characteristics of school and by the school's relations to the society at large. Bricker's argument emphasizes the importance of cooperative learning. I find that, to a significant extent, my students do not wish to engage in cooperative learning. They want to do their own work. On those rare occasions when students ask if they can do a joint project, I almost always end up discussing grading. (I am required to give them a grade.) If they are to do joint work, I must give them a common grade, regardless of who makes the greatest contribution, or else they must do their work in a way that makes it clear to me who is responsible for what. These conditions are difficult to meet. To some degree and at all levels, our individual-ized manner of work in schools is driven by the grading system. Teachers who wish to emphasize cooperative learning will find themselves in a constant battle to devise ways in which they can assign individual responsibility to student performance.

Of course, a response to this might be that the grading system is itself nothing more than a different manifestation of the commit-ment to liberal egalitarianism. In our society we must ultimately succeed or fail for ourselves. We do not get jobs or earn our living as groups. And if we must succeed or fail as a consequence of our own merit, we must also be evaluated for our own work. Or at least we are likely to think so. The structural characteristics of schools are thus liberal sentiments writ large.

But, so one structuralist argument goes, these very liberal political sentiments are themselves requirements of a capitalist society. People must believe that they own themselves or at least their labor if their labor is to be treated as a commodity to be exchanged in free markets. They must believe that they succeed or fail as a result of their own effort if the dominance of capital over their lives is to be adequately hidden. Thus, at heart, our political ideas are driven by the requirements of our economic system. It is this, and not our ideologies themselves, that is fundamental in how we organize work in schools. Ideas do not drive practice. Instead practice drives ideas.

Bricker's work thus raises larger issues. Granted, educational practice is generated by our political conceptions, inarticulate or otherwise. But do these political conceptions originate from an autonomous intellectual tradition in which free men and women have sought to understand how best to govern themselves and to structure their social lives, or do they merely express and legitimate economic arrangements that have their sources independently of our reflective lives? Bricker's work assumes the former view. I am inclined to agree. But a higher level of articulateness about our political life is required if we are to resist simply believing what is convenient for us to believe, given current interests and divisions of power in our society.

The second central theme in this book is the dialogue between a liberal and a communitarian view. This debate is rapidly becoming central to the arguments between political philosophers. Roughly, the argument is this: Communitarians argue that liberals, in their quest to defend individual liberty, have begun to dissolve the bonds of community. Liberal freedom has resulted in a lonely and individuated self, united to others only by agreements struck for the sake of self interests. The sole ethic of this self is the requirements of justice. Justice spells out the rules according to which individuals compete with one another to realize their own freely chosen ends. Liberal justice is thus Hobbes' war of all against all made civilized because it is conducted according to rules. Even the more leftist views of liberal justice such as that of John Rawls involve such a conception. Rawls' "difference principle" requires that we organize our economic affairs to the benefit of the least advantaged. We must do so in order to show equal respect for their status as persons. But here we are motivated by duty. We owe justice to everyone, but friendship and generosity to no one. We need not care for the least advantaged. Justice requires respect for the moral law, not caring for people.

Communitarians object to this caricature of liberalism in several ways. I shall note two. First, they claim that liberalism denies the grounding of the self in community. People are not born as autonomous and unencumbered selves free to shop for their ends in some valuational cafeteria. They are born into communities where they become, not liberal selves, but members of particular human communities. In learning the values and practices of their communities, they are constituted as selves. As they become conscious and reflective, they discover that they are encumbered selves. They discover that they already have ends and commitments. They have them by virtue of the accidents of their birth and the human associations and cultural resources that are part of their particular communities. When liberals insist on the autonomy of individuals to be the authors of their own lives and, indeed, of their own selves, they shear people of their particularity, their ties to their fellow human beings and of their grounding in society. In short, liberal conceptions of freedom and autonomy divest people of that which makes them human.

The second alleged failure of liberalism is that it rejects the moral significance of what might be called the goods of community. Liberalism, at least in its deontological form, provides two basic grounds for people to treat one another justly. First, there is respect for persons. We must treat one another as ends instead of means. Second, we must respect the moral law. Liberals thus are to be motivated to right action by respect for abstract "personhood" and by duty.

Communitarians rightly suggest that such abstract motives are unlikely to actually motivate very many real people. Recall the quip, "Of course I love humankind; it's people I can't stand." Duty and respect for persons often do not triumph over the more concrete motives that spring from our ordinary human activities and associations. Communitarians give us more tangible motives. They are rooted in the goods we seek to accomplish in association with others.

Consider the case of team sports. Athletes are motivated by their concern for the point of the game. At its best this means not only to win, but to play well. The genuine sportsman is motivated to display the excellences of the sport. Often in a team sport one result is friendship for the members of one's team and, indeed, a camaraderie with all those who share the sport. Last year, I spent a long weekend canoe camping in New York State's Adirondack Park. I recall a pleasant conversation on the art of catching brook trout with a man I met at the outlet of a small stream. We shared places to fish, good lures (lure lore), and our respect for the deviousness of trout. And we bemoaned the effects of acid rain on the fishing. Here was a person with whom I had a natural affinity. But I must note that his mangled grammar and limited vocabulary also suggested that he was poorly educated. He was the sort of person I am unlikely to meet or to share my time with apart from the mountain streams and the fish. But there we sought common goals and valued common excellences. Thus he was a friend for a brief interlude.

Liberalism, communitarians may hold, has little place for such motives in its moral theory. Communitarians are likely to see them as central to its ethical concerns. People are motivated by the common purposes of their communities and by a desire to achieve and to exhibit the excellences that are required to pursue these purposes. Moreover, the common pursuit of goals and excellences develops desirable human relations, friendship, generosity, solidarity, caring. These goods of community are experienced as intrinsically worthwhile, but they are also what motivates us to treat one another well. These goods of community are far more likely to motivate us to treat people ethically than are respect for persons and care. Thus, in dissolving the bonds of community, liberalism undermines much that is valuable in human life, and it undermines the motivation for humane treatment of others. Liberalism can easily become a war of all against all conducted according to rules that no one is much motivated to obey.

Liberals, of course, are not without response to such claims. They may point out that it is one thing to choose to belong to a community, but a far different thing to have one's identity submerged in it. I may choose to fish, and I may be a member of the community of those who fish. Liberals would not deny me the goods of community when I choose to pursue them. But I can also decide to do something else. I can come in out of the rain, not keep on casting when the fish are not biting, think about philosophy while I wait for the fish to bite. In short, I can distance myself from this role, put it on when it suits and take it off when it does not. I am not linked to it or absorbed in it in such a way that I must always think and act as a fisherman. Liberals insist that part of freedom is to have this kind of distance from one's role or one's community, and they accuse communitarians of merging people too firmly into their roles and communities. They also may point out that communities differ in their educational capacity. Some may offer wide ranging possibilities for growth. Others may be limited or even perverse. Bizarre religious sects and Nazis form communities too. Are we to extol their virtues to those who find their selves encumbered with the commitments of such communities? Likewise liberals might note that those motives for ethical conduct that spring from community associations often do not apply to those outside of the fold. How am I to meet my Adirondack friend when he is not fishing? Is he now an outsider to whom I owe no duties? May I treat him as I please because he is no longer a member of my group? Communitarian motives may be more powerful than liberal motives, but they are parochial, not universal.

And yet there is something appealing to the call of community. Can we be liberals with a communitarian edge? David Bricker suggests that this is possible. His argument has three crucial features.

First, Bricker suggests a sensible relationship between the goods of community and the demands of liberal justice. It is a good thing when people are able to govern their interactions by the goods of community. In families, friendships, or close-knit groups, people may deal with one another motivated by love, friendship, generosity, or a concern for shared ends. A concern for justice may recede into the background. Where the goods of community prevail, no one need think of liberal justice or be moved by abstract duties. In such circumstances, justice functions as a minimum standard, something that becomes important when the goods of community break down or when they are not there at all. Justice tells us how we must treat those to whom we are bound by no deep ties. It is thus not the sum total of morality. It is our moral safety net. We are thus free to seek the goods of community within the bounds of liberal justice.

Second, Bricker argues that we are grounded in society. We become human by being initiated into various "forms of life." Our humanity depends on our internalizing the forms of acting and thinking that have been developed by other human beings. Thus, it is true that we come to consciousness as encumbered selves, not as empty selves with a life to choose from a myriad of possibilities. But Bricker insists that autonomy is nevertheless a central good. If we are to be free, we need to learn how to distance ourselves from our encumbrances so that we may choose among them. Autonomy is not so much the capacity to choose goods for the self as it is the capacity to judge the goods one finds one's self to have, to keep those that seem fitting, to discard those that do not, and to choose others. Autonomy is not so much the capacity to create one's self as it is the capacity to *recreate* one's self. To do this it is necessary that we achieve a certain degree of distance from our ends. We must treat them more as possessions of the self than as constituents of the self. Until we learn to have this distance we cannot but be what we have been made by others.

Finally, and I think most interestingly, Bricker holds that the goods of community, particularly generosity, provide the best motivation for practices that lead to autonomy. I would state the claim more broadly. Perhaps a variety of liberal values are best sought for children indirectly by first seeking the goods of community. Bricker's argument is that generosity is the best motive for cooperative learning and that cooperative learning can aid the development of autonomy. I think that this is correct. Yet there may also be a larger point about moral motivation to be made here.

I have suggested above that liberalism does not deal well with motivational issues. Many modern liberals are reluctant to appeal to self-interest as a motivation for just behavior. Yet what seems left to them is an appeal to abstract notions such as respect for persons or for the moral law. Such motives seem excessively abstract even for adults. That an appeal to them is easily made to children seems even more doubtful. How then are we to teach children to value justice?

Bricker presents part of a theory of moral socialization, one that is basically Aristotelian in its character although Bricker takes it from a version provided by Paul Taylor. The essence of Aristotle's view was that moral education begins in habituation. Children begin to learn to be just or to act virtuously by being gotten to act in ways that are just or virtuous. As they are habituated to such acts, and as they learn to talk about them and think about them in the way that they are talked about and thought about in the community, they come to acquire the motives or feelings that are appropriate to such acts and to begin to see their point. Finally as they mature, they may learn to fully appreciate the reasons for just or virtuous behavior and to be able to rationally appraise their motives and their conduct.

I would add to this picture the view that liberal motives such as respect for persons and respect for the moral law are likely to begin in the moral sentiments acquired through being taught to act in family or community. Such motives begin with caring in the family where children are (it is to be hoped) not only cared for, but taught to behave in caring ways toward other family members. This caring may be expanded into generosity as the child moves into larger social contexts and is taught to exhibit generous behavior. Schools are obvious places to accomplish the transfer to a larger group of moral sentiments and patterns of behavior that begin in the family. At the end of this process, students may have learned to respect the value of all persons and may have acquired patterns of behavior that they regard as moral duties. At each stage in this transformation, if it goes as hoped, people learn to attach moral sentiments to a larger group of people and to identify those to whom these moral sentiments are attached by a more abstract and less parochial set of criteria. Thus, what may begin as love or caring in the family may become friendship for acquaintances, generosity to classmates, and concern for the members of the community or the nation, and may end as respect for persons as such. Likewise habits of virtuous or just conduct may be more deeply understood by being subsumed under an increasingly abstract set of rules until there is created an abstract sense of justice and a moral response to duty.

This does not mean that respect for persons is simply caring or generosity directed equally toward everyone. The cognitive structure of motives will evolve as their objects change. Moreover, caring, generosity, or friendship will continue to be a part of people's lives in a way that is different from duty, respect for persons, and justice. The goods of community will be felt more intensely and will be applied to a more particularized group of people. They will also be non-obligatory. Caring and love may continue for family, friendship for those to whom we feel some special bond, and generosity for those whom we frequently and personally encounter. It does not follow that those who have never been taught to care or to be generous will be capable of respect for persons, of a sense of duty, or of just behavior. The more abstract moral motives must be developed from the more natural moral sentiments.

What David Bricker has provided in this book is one line of argument that suggests that the goods of community and the practices that foster community may be important for the development of capacities and values that are important to liberals. I believe that he is right, and I have sketched above some additional reasons why one might believe him. If he is right, his work constitutes a profound critique of the practice of schools which liberals must consider. Arguably, current practice justifies much of the communitarian critique of liberalism. Students work as though they are isolated individuals. The goods of community are not encouraged. Students are taught as though they are apprentice soldiers in the war of all against all, civilized by rules. Perhaps they are taught this way because ultimately that is how we really see how things are. If so, we need to reassert the goods of community in schools. And we may need to do so even if we are more liberals than communitarians. For it may turn out that students who are taught as though they are apprentice soldiers in the war of all against all will fail to develop the autonomy that liberals rightly prize, and they may even fail to learn to respect the rules that civilize the war.

David Bricker has written an excellent book that addresses a part of a profound agenda. Those who aspire to more for our children than that they become successful economic soldiers in the war of all against all, those who hope that children might grow into autonomous, morally responsible people, good citizens, and people to whom the goods of community are of worth, will do well to consider it carefully.

KENNETH A. STRIKE
CORNELL UNIVERSITY

Preface

In this book I aim to connect teachers' widely held concerns that they be fair to certain foundational ideas in liberal political theory. I have long been convinced that the problems teachers encounter as they try to coordinate their duties to motivate students and to evaluate students' work are linked to an underlying complexity in the conception, used in liberal accounts of politics, of what makes up a person. Therefore, I have sought to bring out connections between the ways teachers think about students as individuals, and the basic entitlements accorded to persons by rights-based, or liberal, political theory. My hope is that the linkage may serve as a shared starting place for teacher-practitioners and political philosophers as together they investigate the kind of self-understanding that is best for citizens of a liberal democracy, and the way such self-understanding can best be evoked in light of the constraints and opportunities encountered by young people in school classrooms.

Political philosophers need, I believe, to attend to the actual processes of political socialization through which students learn, not only from what they explicitly read and hear, but also from how they are indirectly permitted by authorities to interact with each other as they focus on the assigned materials. Additionally, teachers need to learn how to connect their view of their own mission as professionals to ideas that are ordinarily of special interests to political theorists and ethicists. I hope that my characterizations of what goes on in schools will help persuade teachers that I am addressing the world that they know. I also hope that my use of Kant's conception of a person will confirm to political theorists that my analysis is indeed grounded in liberal theory of political conduct. If I succeed in addressing and linking the special interests of practitioners as well as of theorists, perhaps that will encourage more cooperation among members of the two groups as they investigate the foundations and methods of civic education. I will be grateful if this book serves as a stimulus for reflection among people who have not before seen that their special fields of interest bear on each other.

This short book was in gestation for over seven years, and during that time I received help and encouragement from many people. Carol, my wife, was always delighted to hear me report any slight progress, and read loyally the stream of drafts. Among my colleagues at Oakland University, Marc Briod, Donald Morse, Richard Burke, and Michael Morden helped me to extricate myself from confusions of my own making. Andy Hargreaves of The Ontario Institute for Studies in Education encouraged me early on to attend to how teachers think about their work and how their thinking reflects their political ideals. Bruce Harker, formerly a colleague and now an international development specialist in Indonesia, helped me to see that there is much to be made of the problems teachers encounter as they treat students as both equals and unequals. Joel Fink, another former colleague, who now serves his country as an elementary school principal, shared with me in the early stages of the project his acute sense of how life in classrooms actually unfolds. Finally, Ruth Rounds has, somehow, managed to transform my scribblings into handsome pages of typed prose. Copyeditor Myra Cleary took on that prose, and through fine craft work managed to untangle some of its worst knots. The remaining infelicities came from my own hand. Without the Oakland University research fellowship that I received in 1983, the gestation period would probably have been even longer.

This book is dedicated to my two sons because they have had to cope with schools that were not nearly as decent as I would have liked them to be. Sorry and bothered about that, I concluded that some recompense might come from thinking about how to make schools more decent for others who will follow after them.

CHAPTER 1

Students' Self-Conception
Developed from Classroom Life

In our nation's schools, young people learn about citizenship. Much of what they learn comes to them indirectly as they draw out ideas about how people should conduct themselves in public, from the ways their teachers manage classroom life. Teachers have been heard to make comments such as: "Bill, please keep quiet and don't bother Jim while he is finishing his assignment." "Yes, Mary, it's OK to help Carla now that you have finished your work." "Come on, Sam, find an idea of your own." When teachers give directions, they usually regard themselves as promoting achievement in academic subjects like math, history, and literature, not as teaching students about citizenship. But it is from comments like the ones above that students acquire an understanding of the rights and responsibilities they have as persons at work in a public place among other persons.

The topic of this book is the *citizenship* that is learned indirectly by students in our nation's schools. I am especially interested in the notions about citizenship that youth draw from the ways they are permitted to treat each other as they try to learn what is being taught to them. The way students are directed to go about their studies is looked upon by some researchers as the "hidden curriculum" of the classroom, "hidden" because it is often not viewed, by either teachers or the public, as a significant source of insight into how people ought to conduct themselves in public. On the other hand, a few researchers have grasped the importance of the hidden curriculum and have striven to make it known to others for whom it is pretty much invisible. For example, in *On What Is Learned in Schools* (1968), Robert Dreeben throws light on the way the idea of personal "merit" is made operational in classrooms, while Philip Jackson, in *Life in Class-rooms* (1968), is attentive to the way immersion in the conventional role of "student" affects one's expectations of others. Despite the contribution of researchers like Dreeben and Jackson, many teachers and others do not yet see the importance of the hidden curriculum and continue to regard studying in classrooms as no more than a means to the goal of individual academic achievement. However, the activity of studying in a social place like school is more than a means to a goal. Organized studying in classrooms is itself a source of messages to students about how they should live together. Schooling provides civic education even when its content is not explicitly civic. I am interested in the civic education provided by the hidden curriculum of classrooms, and I am concerned that this education be made humane and noble.

To a considerable degree, citizenship in classrooms is a matter of learning how to defer to the requirements of ownership: Bill is told to leave Jim alone until he finishes *his* assignment; Mary is given permission to help Carla because she has finished *her* work; and Sam is told to develop *his own* idea. The idea of ownership, or of possession, is a fundamental part of our conception of citizenship in a capitalistic democracy. If we were to remove the idea so that it could no longer inform our conception of what we should be doing as we live together in our public places, we would have transformed our citizenship into something very different. No longer would it be possible for people to pursue employment on the basis of their own talents. No longer would people be able to acquire their own possessions. Life as we know it would no longer be possible. Indeed, none of us could live his or her *own* life at all.

I will examine the way the idea of possession is used by teachers as they manage their classrooms. I choose to make the idea of possession the focal point of my investigations because I am worried by some of the uses to which it is being put. The idea of possession serves to protect people from each other: For example, "Stop twisting that arm; it's my arm," or "That's my idea and I deserve credit for it." The idea of possession serves as a moral barrier behind which people can retreat when they are put upon by aggressors. But it should be observed that the protection that people enjoy on the basis of possession involves their individuation from each other. Protected, they stand alone, separated from each other, each connected to his or her possessions, each obligated not to violate the possessions of others. I worry that respect for the individuations brought about by possession seduces teachers into neglecting the social virtues that serve to connect persons to each other. I have in mind virtues like friendship and generosity. In friendship and generosity, people adopt the interests of other persons as their own interests. I believe that the citizenship implied by the hidden curriculum cannot be humane and noble until respect for individuated persons is augmented by the devotion of individuated persons to the social virtues.

I would not want students to infer from the hidden curriculum that they should ignore one another out of respect for possession, yet one of the lessons Philip Jackson finds students receiving from their time in classrooms is that others are to be ignored.

> Another aspect of school life, related to the general phenomena of distractions and interruptions, is the recurring demand that the student ignore those who are around him. In elementary classrooms students are frequently assigned seatwork on which they are expected to focus their individual energies. During these seatwork periods talking and other forms of communication between students are discouraged, if not openly forbidden. The general admonition in such situations is to do your own work and leave others alone. (Jackson, 1968, 16)

I am worried about the cumulative impact that ignoring others has upon the civic imagination of young people. I do not want young people to believe that to be a good citizen one must simply stay within one's own morally protected space—that space prescribed by the idea of possession—and never to serve others or join with others. A society in which citizens always stand at a distance from each other because they fear that joining might violate someone's right of possession would not be a decent society. Yet I have reason to believe that is precisely how students perceive citizenship in our nation's classrooms.

In the course of writing a book on the condition of our nation's schools, John Goodlad had observers visit all kinds of schools, from one coast to the other, north and south, large and small, rural, suburban, and urban (Goodlad, 1984, 16–28). On the basis of the reports sent back by his observers, Goodlad concluded that in most school classrooms most students spend most of their time studying alone (105–06). Think about that. Imagine 25 or 50 students—regardless of their age—seated in a classroom learning the same subject at the same time. For the most part, they study and learn alone. They may overhear one another asking their teacher questions, and during class discussions they may address each other. But when it comes time to do their assignments, they typically work alone. Seldom do they help each other or collaborate. Usually they are told by their teacher to concentrate on doing their own best work by working alone.

The idea of possession is basic to a liberal conception of a human being and to the principle of equal opportunity for individual human beings, which liberals derive from that conception. For example, consider sociologist Daniel Bell's analysis of "equal opportunity."

> The principle of equality of opportunity derives from a fundamental tenet of classic liberalism: that the individual—and not the family, the community, or the state—is the basic unit of society, and that the purpose of societal arrangements is to allow the individual freedom to fulfill his own purposes—by his labor to gain property, by exchange to satisfy his wants, by upward mobility to achieve a place commensurate with his talents. It was assumed that individuals will differ—in their natural endowments, in their energy, drive, and motivation, in their conception of what is desirable—and that the institutions of society should establish procedures for regulating fairly the competition and exchanges necessary to fulfill these diverse desires and competencies. (Bell, 1972, 40)

Bell brings out the liberal belief that individuals morally are more basic, that is, more important than society, and as part of this basic status, they are equipped with *their* endowments, *their* energy, *their* conception of what is desirable. Yet all persons as "basic units" are members of social groups, such as families, communities, and states. Young persons acquire habits and perspectives from their surrounding groups, and Bell draws the liberal distinction between a person and a group in such a way that young persons' socially acquired traits do not belong to them in the same way that their endowments, energy, and conception of the desirable do. With the distinction between person and group in mind, educators easily arrive at the conclusion—which is a liberal interpretation of educational justice—that it would be unjust for young students to be held back by their socially acquired traits because the traits are not theirs. If students are to be held back at all, it should be only because of their endowments and energy, not because of their social traits.

In the following pages, I investigate the relationship between the liberal theory of possession and the fact that in our nation's classrooms most students study alone. I appreciate that teachers have nonmoral reasons for having students work alone. Students are immature, and in their immaturity they often would rather dawdle with their friends than concentrate on assignments. Also, they can be intolerant and unkind toward those whom they regard as outsiders. Teachers who prefer to have students do their assignments alone may be trying to avoid the chaos that they fear would result from the freedom to collaborate with classmates. I worry, though, that the short-run, tactical advantages gained by having students work alone come at the expense of broader moral benefits. I worry that our students are learning that being a good citizen is primarily a matter of staying out of other people's right-of-way. I am concerned about the moral adequacy of the conception of citizenship that students are drawing out of their immersion in classroom life and the bearing that the conception has upon their self-understanding.

When I speak of "liberals" I do not mean those who stand opposite "conservatives" on an axis of political dispute. I am not speaking of Democrats as opposed to Republicans, of Ted Kennedy as opposed to Jack Kemp. According to my present usage, a "liberal" is a person who believes that all people are equal as moral subjects and that, in their equality, they possess the same rights to life, liberty, and the pursuit of happiness (Gray, 1986, x). The "liberal" to whom I am referring harbors a distinctive combination of beliefs about persons as moral subjects and, in light of these beliefs, infers that fairness or justice is the first virtue of public life. All persons—Democrats and Republicans alike—who hold these beliefs are "liberals" in this sense.

The belief that all young people have a right to equal educational opportunity and that teachers are obligated by that right to justly distribute benefits and burdens among students implies that all persons are morally equal despite their many physical differences. The belief that the physical differences between persons have no bearing on their status as equal moral subjects receives much of its philosophical support from the work of Immanuel Kant. Kant theorizes that among moral and political ideals, justice, or fairness, comes first (Kant, 1959, 17). The philosopher Michael Sandel says that the belief that justice, or fairness, is first in public life is the civic belief of "deontological liberals," a "formidable name" he coins for the "familiar doctrine" that "society, being composed of a plurality of persons, each with his own aims, interests, and conceptions of the good, is best arranged when it is governed by principles that do not *themselves* presuppose any particular conception of the good" (Sandel, 1982, 1).

Sandel himself is critical of the conception of a person as a moral subject, which is favored by those like Kant and the contemporary political philosopher John Rawls, who hold that justice is the primary principle of public life. For example, Sandel complains that Rawls' person is fundamentally an individuated moral unit for whom affiliation with others is only one possible alternative way of life, with some form of solitary living being another alternative (Sandel, 1982, 62). Sandel argues, in opposition to Rawls, that affiliation is fundamental to our humanity, not just an alternative we are free to accept or reject.

I have been much stimulated and enlightened by the way Sandel treats competing conceptions of a person as the ultimate point of dispute between the "deontological liberals," whom he criticizes, and the communitarian theorists, with whom he sympathizes. In large part because of Sandel's influence, I have made the conception of a person, especially the role played in the conception by the idea of possession, the primary object of my attention and the unifying theme of this book. Nevertheless, Sandel has not persuaded me to join the communitarian critics of deontological liberalism, because I do not think it would be wise to give up the individual protections that deontological liberals so strongly affirm. I view myself, therefore, as a deontological liberal, but a *restrained* deontological liberal. I value the contributions made by nonobligatory virtues like friendship and generosity to the quality of public life, even though I accept justice as the first principle of that life and therefore regard persons as morally protected and individuated. In the following pages, I show that I still can derive from my deontological convictions reasons for recommending that the hidden curriculum be made congenial to acts of generosity and friendship. Broadly speaking, I would like the virtues of friendship and generosity to permeate public life to such a degree that a preoccupation with justice, that is, a preoccupation that people get what they deserve, is not the ever-present concern of citizens. I look upon the principle of justice and the right to individual protections that it implies as ideally a fallback position, a "safety net" for the regulation of human beings when their friendship and generosity fail. I would not want to live in a community where there were no such safety net, yet I could not regard as humane and noble communities where people were continuously preoccupied with everyone's getting what they deserved and nothing more.

To repeat, I have been and remain concerned about the civic education that young people are being given by the hidden curriculum in classrooms. I am responding to that concern by investigating the morality of the hidden curriculum. As a restrained deontological liberal, I would like to put justice in its proper place theoretically as one part of the hidden curriculum by incorporating into the curriculum collaborative learning motivated by friendship and generosity. I will put the principle of justice in its proper place by using it as a starting point for an argument that will conclude that friendly collaboration should be encouraged in classrooms. More specifically, I will concentrate on the conception of a person as viewed by supporters of liberal justice and will show that collaboration is needed so that the hidden curriculum may allow for the development of self-understanding among students in a way that complies with that conception.

The fulfillment of obligations and the practice of nonobligatory virtues constitute two different kinds of moral activity. Even though as a restrained deontological liberal I agree that basic duties, such as the duty to be just, are more critical to our humanity than is the practice of social virtues, I will show how the conception of a person, according to liberal justice, can be used to endorse nonobligatory, social virtues for the public realm. My argument is an endeavor to uncover a connection between two kinds of moral experience which some ethicists look upon as being disconnected from each other (Frankena, 1973, 10). They maintain that friendship and generosity are appropriate in family-like groups, where people know each other well yet have the option to leave if the friendship evaporates. They also maintain that the principle of justice is binding upon persons who meet one another as strangers in the public spaces of their society.[1] I plan to show that justice in public school classrooms needs to be augmented by friendship and generosity so that young people can achieve the self-understanding and independence called for by the conception of a person that makes the justice intelligible.

Simply put, justice is the distribution of benefits and burdens among persons according to what they each deserve. According to deontological liberalism, justice is an irrevocable obligation, not a matter of discretion, not something a person can choose to ignore without vulnerability to moral censure. On the other hand, social virtues such as friendliness and generosity are not general obligations: I have no general obligation to be friendly toward anyone, nor am I obligated to be generous to anyone. Morally, I am free to be friendly and generous toward as many, or as few, persons as I choose. While we would have a difficult time admiring a person who was neither friendly nor generous toward anyone, we could not censure such a Scrooge for failure to fulfill an obligation.

Friendliness and generosity involve caring about the well-being of other persons. Their well-being becomes a matter of personal concern so that we believe that our own lives flourish when theirs flourish and that by contributing to their well-being we contribute to our own. This is not to say that friendliness and generosity are simply disguised selfishness, that we are friendly and generous simply to gratify ourselves. Although fulfillment of the motive is usually accompanied by pleasure and satisfaction, the motive is to help someone else, not oneself (Hospers, 1982, 76–77).

Think of yourself as the host or hostess of a dinner party. The time has come for you to serve a scrumptious dessert to your guests. Are you going to serve it generously or justly? If you serve the dessert generously, you will consider the well-being of your guests. How about Jim, seated on your right? You know that Jim craves strawberries—the dessert is full of them—but you also know that Jim is dieting, and your dessert is heavy on calories. So you decide to give Jim a moderate serving, not as much as he would like, but more than you are giving Susan, Jim's wife. You know that Susan doesn't care for strawberries very much, so she would not enjoy a large serving. But she would not like to be made conspicuous by not being served anything, so you serve her just enough to permit her to keep up the pretence that she is enjoying her meal, even though this part of the meal is not a favorite of hers. Then there is Craig, Sherri's husband, who is next to Susan. Craig is fit as a fiddle, so Craig can have a large serving without harm. You heap the dessert on Craig's plate.

Note that as you generously served your dessert, you gave no thought to what your guests deserved. You did not think of yourself as the subject of their claims upon you to award them servings proportionate to their individual merit. What they merit was not a matter of concern. Instead, you were thinking of each of them as a friend, people whom you entertain because you have grown to care about them as individual personalities, not because you view your relationship with them as a matter of justice. Michael Sandel, the critic of the deontological liberals' conviction that justice is the foundation of public life, argues that transforming relationships into just relationships does not necessarily constitute a moral improvement (Sandel, 1982, 33). It would be an improvement, he says, if the prior relationships were unjust. But if the prior relationships were expressive of friendliness and generosity, then their transformation into just relationships would be a transition from one worthy moral practice to another, equally worthy practice.

Sandel gives the example of a family where friendliness and generosity prevail (Sandel, 1982, 33). The family members care about one another as individuals; they assist each other because they care, with no thought about whether or not they are receiving "just" compensation in return. Then, their relationships are transformed, and concern for justice comes to prevail. No longer do the family members provide for one another because they care; now, they provide because they each understand themselves to be obligated to provide, and the aim of their living together now is that they each obtain no more or no less than a fair share. Sandel's insight is that such a transformation would involve a qualitative change in the family relationships, but not a qualitative improvement.

I have briefly surveyed the difference between fulfilling a general obligation like the obligation to be just, and practicing a social virtue. That difference will be important for my inquiry. Currently, liberal philosophers like John Rawls and communitarian philosophers like Michael Sandel are addressing each other as if their theories rest upon conceptions of a person that are fundamentally at odds. I will try to show that the liberal conception of a person can be used to endorse a kind of hidden curriculum that may teach youth the social virtues of special interest to communitarians. Social scientists like Robert Dreeben and Talcott Parsons write as if virtues like friendliness and generosity have little place in public settings where people face each other as strangers (Dreeben, 1968, Chap. 3; Parsons, 1968, 69–90). In contrast, I believe that in decent communities friendliness and generosity should not be restricted to exchanges between family members within their homes. In my inquiry I plan to connect theoretically liberal and communitarian moral priorities as well as to explain how such a connection could be put to practice in schools. Using the liberal principle of justice as my starting point, I plan to argue that friendliness and generosity should be evoked from students because practicing these virtues helps them achieve a type of self-understanding that is faithful to the conception of a person according to the principle of justice itself.

Students' life in classrooms is echoed in their understanding of who they are as public persons living in a nation that accepts the protected moral subject and, correlatively, accepts justice as the foundation of public morality. It is therefore important that the hidden curriculum of classrooms cause students to understand themselves as public persons in keeping with the conception of a moral subject as implied by the principle of justice. But does that faithfulness require that the hidden curriculum reflect justice alone? Does the concept of a person, according to the principle of justice, leave no room for generosity between public persons? I plan to show that in the spirit of justice there is a need for generous exchanges between citizens.

At the time he wrote "Ducks vs. Hard Rocks" Deairich Hunter was a junior in a Wilmington, Delaware high school. For four months that year he had lived in Brooklyn, New York and had attended public high school there. In Brooklyn he met types of students whom he had never met in Wilmington, and wrote his essay for his classmates back home so that they might have some idea of life in an inner-city school. "Ducks" is Hunter's label for the Brooklyn students who "go to school every day" and who take their grades seriously because they want to go to college. But Hunter observed that most of the Brooklyn students were "hard rocks" or "junkies." "Hard rocks" have "no worries, no cares" about school; they often play hookey. The "junkies" operate as loners and would "stab you in the back" to get money for one more "fix." Toward the end of his short essay Hunter speculates on what would be needed for the "hard rocks" to become serious about school.

> I guess the best way to help the hard rocks is to help the ducks. If the hard rocks see the good guy making it, maybe they will change. If they see the ducks, the ones who try, succeed, it might bring them around. The ducks are really the only ones who might be able to change the situation. (Hunter, 1985, 68)

Here, Hunter is looking at the Brooklyn school from the perspective of an outsider, who briefly was a part of its student body. From his vantage point as an outsider he sees that the imagination of the Brooklyn students has been limited by the traditions of their school. Traditionally, students care only about themselves: "Ducks" never care about "hard rocks."

In the final paragraph of his essay Hunter places himself among the "ducks."

> The problem with most ducks is that after years of effort they develop a negative attitude, too. If they succeed, they know they've got it made. Each one can say he did it by himself and for himself. No one helped him and he owes nobody anything, so he says, "Let the hard rocks and the junkies stay where they are"—the old every-man-for-himself routine. . . .
> Maybe the only people left with hope are the only people

who can make a difference—teens like me. We, the ducks, must learn to care. As a fifteen-year-old, I'm not sure I can handle all that. Just growing up seems hard enough. (Hunter, 1985, 68)

Hunter glimpses that in order for schools to become more decent places for everyone, he and other "ducks" must learn how to care for those students who find school exasperating. Yet, he ends, "I'm not sure I can handle all that."

Just like the imagination of the students about whom he writes, Hunter's own moral imagination reflects the custom that students not care for one another: The custom is that they just do their own work and let the others take care of themselves. The effect of the hidden curriculum upon the moral imagination of students like Deairich Hunter disturbs me. I do not believe that it is the kind of civic education that is needed for decent living in our nation.

Chapter 2 highlights the contribution of the idea of possession to a liberal conception of a person. Briefly, possession is a normative relationship achieved by voluntary agents when they approve of some alternative for themselves. Because of the requirement for approval, individual autonomy is necessary for possession. In Chapter 2 I use a liberal conception of a person to develop one possible justification for having students work alone in classrooms. That justification is that when students work alone there is less of an operational conflict for teachers between two activities mandated by fairness, those of motivating all students to learn and of informing them about how well their learning matches up with standards of academic excellence. If teachers were to reduce the conflict between student equality and academic excellence, then they might get their students to learn more, and that learning would enhance the individual autonomy that is necessary for a possessive relationship.

In Chapter 3 I explain what is wrong with the justification for studying independently that I developed in the preceding chapter. My purpose here is to show that the theory of liberal individualism is wrongly practiced by routinely having students work alone in order that they may do their own work. It is wrongly practiced, I argue, because the routine gives students false clues about their relationship with their school work. The misunderstandings that arise from the false clues simply delay their achievement of autonomy, which is one of the major aims of the practice of teaching students fairly. I use Wittgenstein's theory of knowledge as a social partnership to make my own liberal argument for periodically involving students in collaborative studying and explain that the clues about knowledge that they receive from collaborating will enhance their chances of becoming autonomous.

After showing that teachers who practice the principles of liberal individualism should occasionally use collaborative studying as one of their approaches, I determine the ideal motive for collaborating. The determination occurs in Chapter 4, where I examine four possible motives for collaborating in light of the liberal ideals of human equality and individual freedom. The first two motives are duty based, the third is oriented toward doing good, and the fourth—generosity—is oriented toward helping other people flourish because of regard for them as persons. I determine that generosity best satisfies the liberal requirements of equality and freedom.

Chapter 4 completes the main argument of the book: At that point I will have shown how to use the conception of protected individuals, presupposed by liberal justice, to make a case for collaborative studying inspired by the spirit of generosity toward others. In Chapter 5 I elaborate upon the connection between individual persons and society that underlies my argument. I show that the autonomy that is so important to the argument does not assign to society an exclusively instrumental role for persons, as communitarian critics of liberalism, like Michael Sandel, charge it does. Moreover, I explain why the communitarian conception of a person is wrong in terms of the person–society relationship. Finally, I build upon the theory of knowledge as social partnership, introduced in Chapter 3, in order to bring to light the social dependency behind liberal individuality and the implications of that dependency for civic education in our nation.

CHAPTER 2

Teachers' Liberal Ideals Reflected in Their Talk About Their Work

Once they adopt the view that persons are equally protected, deontological liberals must conclude that people's physical characteristics are not constituents of persons as moral subjects. This is because people are not equal in their characteristics: Some weigh more than others, some are taller than others, and so forth. If deontological liberals were to hold that physical characteristics are constituents of persons as moral subjects, then the equality of the subjects would be lost.

The equality of moral subjects is comprehensible only if we think of there being a distance between persons as subjects and the physical characteristics they carry. But that distance should not be thought of as unlimited. If it were unlimited, moral subjects would be completely unattached to all physical characteristics, and there would be two persons, not one, living in two entirely disconnected realms, a moral realm and a physical realm. The moral person would have the protection, while the physical person would have the capacity to accomplish tasks in the physical realm. But there would be no protected person who also is able to accomplish tasks in the physical realm.

The idea of possession is used by deontological liberals to prevent the distance between moral subjects and physical characteristics from becoming unlimited. They conceive of subjects, for example, as having arms, legs, eyes, and a brain that *belong* to them. The idea of possession both *relates* subjects to physical characteristics and *distances* subjects from the characteristics (Sandel, 1982, 54). It relates by making certain characteristics the characteristics *of* a particular subject, and it distances by introducing the distinction *between* a possessor and that which is possessed.

Deontological liberals do not all agree about the relationship between young moral subjects and the natural endowments they carry. Some, like the liberals to whom Daniel Bell (1972) refers, believe that young subjects *have* natural endowments; others, like John Rawls, deny that individual subjects have endowments, and contend instead that endowments belong to all subjects together as the ingredients of a collectively owned talent pool (Rawls, 1973, 101). As a "restrained" deontological liberal I side with Bell's liberals in this dispute, and in Chapter 4 I will explain why Rawls' theory of collectively owned talent is unsatisfactory. Nevertheless, the distinctions Rawls makes are useful, and I plan to employ some of them. For example, Rawls labels his view—the view that talents belong to everyone collectively—the "democratic egalitarian" view, and he calls the view that Bell's liberals and I hold, the "liberal egalitarian" alternative to his view (Rawls, 1973, 65).

I have acknowledged that I am a deontological liberal who nevertheless wants to put the idea of possession, so important to this liberalism, in its place so that room can be provided for friendship and generosity. More precisely, I am one of two varieties of deontological liberals; I am a liberal egalitarian. As a liberal egalitarian, I hold that natural endowments belong to individual persons, not everyone collectively, yet I deny that socially conditioned attributes of immature persons belong to them (Rawls, 1973, 73). I realize that immature persons carry socially conditioned attributes, but I contend that the attributes are not *theirs*.

Imagine, for example, an eight-year-old girl whose test scores show that she has great aptitude for science and mathematics. Yet, she habitually visits with her friends during science and math periods and in many ways shows indifference toward two subjects in which she is especially talented. During the fall parent conference her teacher hears her parents exclaim that none of their older daughters went on to college; instead, they went right to work. The mother recalls that she got married immediately after high school and started her family. The teacher concludes that the eight-year-old daughter in her class has been exposed all her life to women who do not regard higher education to be a suitable alternative for females and who probably would not approve of any scientific or technical profession for a young woman. The teacher concludes that her young student's reaction to science and mathematics is socially acquired; the girl has learned from the other women in her family that there is no need for females to become seriously engaged in the study of science and math.

If the girl's teacher were a deontological liberal, she would believe that the girl has a right to educational opportunity equal to that of other young people. And if she were a liberal egalitarian practitioner of deontological liberalism, she would also believe that she is correlatively obligated by the girl's right to do everything within her professional competence to motivate the girl to study science and math seriously even though she does not want to. The teacher interprets the girl's not wanting to study as a socially conditioned attitude, an attitude that does not "belong" to her and therefore one for which she is not responsible. Because the attitude does not belong to her, the teacher could not wrong her by trying to "disconnect" her from the attitude, that is, by trying to change the attitude. Furthermore, from the liberal egalitarian point of view, the teacher should try to change that "negative" attitude; otherwise, the science and math education that the girl receives will reflect a socially conditioned attitude that she carries but that is morally arbitrary to her in the sense that it does not belong to her. That would be unfair. It would be unfair to the girl to permit, without any opposition, her negative attitude to limit her performance in science and math. If that were to happen, the girl's family, not the girl herself, would, in Bell's words, be treated as the "basic unit" of morality. In order to treat the *girl* as the basic unit, the liberal egalitarian teacher must try to encouarge attitudes toward study that will lead her to do her best work. The only limit on her best work should be the limit of her natural endowments, not arbitrary limits imposed upon her by her initial starting place in society.

Liberal egalitarian teachers do not just offer educational opportunities to young people and then let them decide whether or not they want to take advantage of the opportunities. Instead, the teachers strive to provide opportunities in ways that will induce reluctant students to learn even though they entered school not wanting to learn. According to liberal egalitarian thinking, being fair to young students is a matter of complying with their right to educational opportunity, and that involves trying to change attitudes that inhibit serious study. Liberal egalitarianism endorses paternalistic teaching: It endorses efforts to remove or transform socially acquired limitations that interfere with a young student's academic achievement (Frankel, 1971, 203–04; Turner, 1960, 862). The goal of liberal egalitarian teaching is that each student do his or her best academic work, work that is proportionate to the individual's natural endowments and that does not reflect the individual's starting place in society and attitudes acquired from that starting place.

In the preceding chapter I explained that I would argue in behalf of collaborative learning inspired by generosity and that the starting point of my argument would be the deontological liberal's conception of a person. I explained that I would speculate on the connection between thinking of persons as possessively connected to individual endowments and the typical absence of collaboration in our nation's classrooms. That speculation follows.

A Liberal Egalitarian Theory of Possession

There need be no physical connection between a person and an object in order for that person to possess that object. For example, imagine a girl named Julie who is using a ball point pen that she does not possess; that is, it is not *her* pen; the pen does not *belong* to her. The pen was lent to Julie by her friend Pam, and it is Pam who possesses the pen, not Julie. However, the watch that Julie left behind on her bedroom dresser today continues to be *her* watch even though the classroom where she is seated is three miles from her home.

Possession is a *normative* relationship, not one of physical connection. This normative relationship gives a possessor the right of first use over that which is possessed. Thus, Julie is the one who has the right of first use over the watch on her dresser; the watch is hers and only hers to use unless she grants permission to someone else to use it. Because Julie has the right of first use over the watch, other persons are obligated to leave the watch alone and to let Julie do with it what she pleases.

Earlier I observed that the idea of possession introduces a distance, but not an unlimited distance, between the possessor and the possessed. That distance is absolutely essential to the intelligibility of liberal egalitarian equality. The liberal egalitarian holds that all persons are equal from the moral point of view. Yet, the natural endowments of equal persons undeniably are unequal. If the unequal endowments were thought of as constituents of persons, then persons would lose their equality. Therefore, there must be some distance between the equal persons and the unequal endowments. However, if that distance were unlimited, the persons would not have any privileged access to the endowments; they would not be able individually to count upon the endowments. The idea of possession limits the distance (Sandel, 1982, 55). The endowments that Julie physically carries are *her* endowments even though they are not constitutive of her. Thus, Julie has the right of first use over the endowments, which means that others should not try to take them away from her or to change them.

Liberal egalitarians concede that adults can be possessively connected to the social attributes they carry, without conceding that young people must be possessively connected as well. They maintain that social attributes can belong to autonomous adults but not to immature persons. Imagine an adult who is a professor of philosophy at a university. A professorship is one of her roles; the role "belongs" to her by legal contract. She and the university came to an agreement based upon the university's assessment of her qualifications and her assessment of the proposed salary and opportunities for collegiality. Now that they have agreed, the role is hers.

People sometimes are impostors and perform roles that are not theirs to perform. The professor of philosophy could put on a white jacket, hang a stethoscope around her neck, and act like a physician. But the role of physician would not really be *her* role because she would not have been approved for it by the appropriate authorities.

Sometimes there is little public agreement concerning the qualifications for performing a role. The professor of philosophy is also Julie's mother. Not only did she give birth to Julie, but she has been caring for Julie since birth. Since Julie is *her* daughter, we can agree that other adults are correlatively obligated not to interfere with her mothering, even though we may disagree about the qualifications of a competent mother.

Since her birth, Julie has learned how to play roles modeled for her by others. Liberal egalitarians would deny that the roles children like Julie learn how to play are *their* roles. Their view is that roles cannot belong to children because children have not yet achieved the critical detachment from the roles they play that is necessary for them to approve of the roles. And such approval is necessary for any role to *belong* to a person. On the other hand, Julie's mother approves of her role of mother; she approves of her role of professor; and by her approval she shows that she understands that she and the roles are not one and the same. She apprehends that she and the roles are different, and she willingly stands behind them. If she did not willingly stand behind a role, the role would not belong to her; for example, a tyrant could capture her and make her one of his slaves, yet the role of slave would not belong to her because she would not have approved it. Roles that are imposed upon persons are not roles to which they are possessively connected, because they had no choice, and possession is based upon choice.

In order for Julie's mother—let's call her Professor Gates—to choose the roles to which she is to become possessively connected, she must grasp the distinction between herself as an agent and the alternative roles available to her. If she did not grasp the distinction, then from her point of view she and the roles would be identical and there would be nothing for her to choose (Sandel, 1982, 56). The ability to differentiate between oneself as an agent and the roles one can play comes with maturation. Young persons are not clear about the distinction; they tend to live their roles rather than play them. Young people cannot be connected to roles by the norm of possession until they become able to detach themselves from roles and to evaluate them. Young people must learn to think of themselves as performers of roles, and not as people for whom roles are integral parts of themselves. Until young people achieve that degree of self-understanding, there can be nothing wrong with a liberal egalitarian teacher's trying to influence them to change roles—for example, from the role of student bully to that of good citizen—because they are not yet possessively connected to their roles. In the absence of possessive connection there is no right of first use that a teacher would violate by trying to teach a student a new role without his or her approval. Later, however, when persons stand behind roles because of the approval they have given to the roles, paternalistic attempts to get them to change would be wrong because the paternalism would violate possession.

Idealism in Teachers' Talk About Their Work

Teachers who practice liberal egalitarian paternalism try to overcome their students' socially produced academic difficulties by providing psychological leadership. The purpose of the leadership is to motivate the students to use their natural endowments—only the endowments possessively connected to them, not the socially acquired handicaps that do not belong to them—to produce their best work. The purpose is to obtain work from students that reflects *them*, not their initial starting place in society. The teachers view the students as morally worthy individuals who have a right to psychological leadership in order that the work they do will be theirs as individual persons, not work that is predictable on the basis of facts concerning their social location.

Teachers echo their moral ideals in their talk about the details of their daily work habits. Consider, for example, some of the things that Verne Vackaro, Jim McGraw, Jim Hall, Donna Duffy, and Jan Heckman say about their teaching. They are all experienced secondary school teachers (Vackaro teaches in a junior high school; the others teach in senior high schools) whom I interviewed twice, first in the fall of 1981 and again in the winter of 1982. The questions that were addressed to all five teachers during the first interview are listed in Appendix A. During the second interview I asked the teachers to elaborate on ideas and approaches that they had mentioned during the first interview, but that I did not think I understood adequately. By doing the second interview I hoped to understand their points of view as accurately and completely as possible.

Teachers seldom have a carefully thought out philosophy of

education that they draw upon to solve the problems of social control and individual motivation that they routinely face. In general, teachers see theory as a distorting simplification of the complex realities of classroom life, so they are pragmatic; by trial and error they develop a repertoire of workable approaches to the routine problems of managing and instructing immature persons (Jackson, 1977, 24). It is in their accounts of their pragmatic approaches that an observer is likely to find indications of the extent of their paternalism toward students.

For example, Vackaro, who teaches social studies, speaks of trying to "keep students alive." Often in his classes he conducts discussions during which he distributes "turns" among students. He describes himself as having several aims in mind as he gives students their turns. "At one time I may be looking to see how extensive the understanding is. Therefore, I might not ask those who have their hands in the air. I might try to find out if it's the same old few who understand or whether it goes deeper. Other times, I might call on people because I want to keep them alive and let them know that they will be called on, and they should be paying attention. That's another function." Vackaro hopes that students will be more likely to stay attentive if they know that he sometimes gives turns randomly. In the above passage he seems to be saying that during discussions he tries to "keep alive" in the minds of all the students the idea that anyone can be called on at any moment. In the second interview Vackaro elaborated, "I call on some people to keep them performing or keep them in discussion." Vackaro went on to explain that students in his classes differ considerably in their abilities, and one of his overriding aims is to lead discussions in a way that makes it possible for a student at any ability level to contribute a useful observation.

Jim McGraw is also a social studies teacher, and in his interviews he explained that in grading daily work he considers the effort behind the work as well as its quality.

> . . . if I'm trying to be fair, that means that I'm taking into consideration the different levels of ability. If I allow a student to sit there and do nothing, then he's not going to be able to demonstrate to me a willingness to do his best. If he doesn't demonstrate a willingness, I'm probably, whether I like it or

not and maybe unconsciously, I'm going to write him off as "sorry, low ability level, not making the effort." That doesn't sound professional, but that's what happens—you write them off because you just don't see the effort coming forth.

McGraw not only wants every one of his students to demonstrate a "willingness" to do his or her best work; he also wants, for the sake of fairness, to evoke that willingness. If the willingness were not forthcoming, little work would be produced, and McGraw might "write the student off." But it would be wrong, it would be unfair, for him to write a student off, so he uses credit for effort as an incentive to keep all students striving to produce their best work, no matter how limited their abilities may be.

Jim Hall, a Spanish teacher, speaks of trying to achieve an acceptable balance between his not "falling down" in his own responsibilities toward his students and his holding students responsible for their actions. He speaks of the responsibility his upper-level students have to do their best.

> If they don't do it [their best], then I don't feel like I have fallen down, I feel that they have. It's a responsibility of theirs since they elected the class to do what is expected of them. That's a very, very important part, I guess, of me personally. That may be because I was a good student in high school. That may be very hard for some of my students that are not good students. They may have trouble with that. I'm not sure.

Hall believes that his upper-level students have more responsibility than the lower-level ones: The lower-level Spanish students are new to learning a foreign language and therefore deserve to have the deadlines for their daily homework enforced more leniently. But the advanced students already have learned that daily practice is essential in learning another language and have assumed greater responsibility for punctual work by freely electing to continue with Spanish. Generally, though, for all students at all levels, Hall tries not to "fall down" by making homework assignments too long, given the students' responsibilities for homework in their other courses. Hall wants to avoid giving any student reason to conclude that it is impossible to do well in one of his

Spanish courses without neglecting responsibilities elsewhere. He wants all of his students to perceive that success in his course is possible. Otherwise, they might give up, and giving up would be a sign that his psychological leadership had failed.

Hall's paternalism is more restrained than Vackaro's and McGraw's: He stresses his and his students' responsibilities about equally, while Vackaro and McGraw put more stress on their own responsibility as professionals to make learning happen. This is not to say that they deny that their students have any responsibility; it is just that they see their immature students as having less responsibility than they, the professionals, have.

The paternalism echoed by Jan Heckman is about as restrained as Hall's. A chemistry teacher, Heckman describes herself as a "liberal" who hopes that her liberalism will "push" students into mastering the material. When asked for an example of how she practices her liberalism, Heckman gave her perspective on make-up tests.

> First of all I'm extremely liberal in letting them hand in late assignments when there's an excused absence. No matter what the parents call an excuse; that's up to the parents to decide. Secondly, if there is an opportunity to retake a test, simply because they were frozen or because they were not quite ready for any reason, I'll always let them retake a test or retake a quiz, or whatever. I feel it's better to have them learn it, even if it is later than everyone else learned it. It's better to have them learn it than just simply say "Well I missed that; too bad" and go on to something else. Particularly when the something else is based on what they didn't learn before.

Heckman is saying that she regards chemistry to be a sequential subject, in which the basics taught first are essential for mastery of the more advanced ideas taught later. The sequential nature of the subject is her reason for providing make-up tests until students achieve an acceptable grade. Otherwise, she says, they would continue on to more advanced material inadequately prepared. Her "pushing" students is not so much a matter of trying to motivate them as it is a matter of trying to give them each enough time to master the basics before going further. She is trying to avoid the demoralizing conclusion that one's situation has become hopeless in the last half of a course because the basic ideas were never learned well in the first half.

Donna Duffy teaches composition and English literature. She emphasizes that the students in her world literature class differ greatly in ability and regards it as her duty to try to motivate them all to read for pleasure and insight. To accomplish this she says that she, like Hall, must achieve a balance: For her it is a balance between having expectations and keeping alive the possibility that even the less able students can achieve some success. "Moderately easy" is her label for her expectations. If her expectations were too low, some students would "just be alive in my class"; if they were too high, some would not have a chance of passing and, understanding their plight, would stop trying: "I could make it [the course] so hard that the kids couldn't pass, and there are teachers doing that, and I can make it so easy, maybe I should say moderately easy, because they don't just have to be alive in my class." For Duffy, the psychological leadership of evoking every student's involvement in a course of study involves a careful calibration of expectations. It also involves her own enthusiasm for writing and literature; she would like to have the following reputation among students:

> As interested and enthusiastic about their learning and about my teaching. I really believe in enthusiasm. I like them to care as much as I do. And also that maybe I taught them something other than book learning. That I gave them a sense of worth.

The enthusiasm that Duffy is speaking about extends beyond writing and literature to the individual students themselves. She hopes that her enthusiasm for them as persons will help each of them experience a "sense of worth," and that from that enhanced sense of worth may come more motivation to study.

I did not tell the teachers whose remarks I am quoting that I would be interested in any evidence of "paternalism" in their thinking: I told them only that I would be asking them to talk about their work. The teachers had opportunities to describe how they approach their daily tasks of grading homework, giving turns during discussions, and helping individuals during seatwork periods. They also had the opportunity at the end of the interview to comment on the meaning of "equal educational opportunity" and the connection, if any, between this broad ideal and their daily work. At no time did I tell any of them about the subject of this book or my conclusions.

Although a paternalistic commitment to arouse students' interest in subjects they would not ordinarily choose to study on their own is found in the teachers' accounts of their approaches to their daily tasks, that commitment virtually disappears when the five teachers reflect upon the broad principle of "equal opportunity." Examine, for instance, the reflections of the three who are most strongly paternalistic in their accounts of their daily work habits:

> I see equal educational opportunity, I see "equal" meaning that every kid is going to be offered a chance for an education. "Opportunity" to me means that you offer them a chance to show you that they're going to succeed at their own level. (McGraw)

> "Equal educational opportunity" I think is meant to indicate that each kid gets a fair chance, that each kid gets an equal opportunity to succeed. (Duffy)

> Well, I don't think it means I have to open my door to anybody who wants to come in. If they're not here to learn, I don't call that "equal educational opportunity." I guess I think equal educational opportunity—anybody who wants to learn will be given within the resources available as much help as they can to go as far as they can. (Vackaro)

McGraw speaks of "offering" a chance; Duffy refers to "giving" students a "fair" chance; and Vackaro mentions "giving" those who are "here to learn" as much help as they need to go "as far as they can." It appears from these general remarks that "equal educational opportunity" is not interpreted by these teachers as mandating the paternalism that they display in their accounts of how they actually teach in their own classrooms. It appears that in their own work they are trying to provide psychological leadership that they think they are not obligated to provide by the broad principle of equal educational opportunity, a principle that many citizens view as the basis for educational justice in the United States.

The contrast between the nonpaternalistic interpretations of equal opportunity and the paternalism echoed in the accounts of daily work habits does not mean that the teachers are providing their paternalistic services frivolously. Rather, they see their efforts at motivating learning as part of being fair to their students. On the other hand, they do not look upon equal opportunity for all students as connected with their own "fairness" to their students: They regard fairness as a basic part of the professional ethics of individual teachers, and they look upon equal opportunity as something to be provided by large educational systems, not by individual teachers. This distinction leaves them free to be nonpaternalistic at the level of a broad principle and paternalistic in their own professional morality.

Early in the first interview I asked the teachers to describe the reputation they "ideally" would like to have among students. All of them except Duffy said they would like to be seen as "fair": "I would like them to view me as fair" (Hall); "My biggest concern is with fairness in the classrooms, and it always has been" (McGraw); "Effective and fair and nice" (Vackaro); "I'm tough but fair" (Heckman). The concern for fairness displayed by these four teachers in their characterizations of their ideal reputation echoes a concern voiced by a larger sample of teachers whom sociologist Dan Lortie interviewed in the early 1960s. Lortie concluded that the frequency with which his teachers mention fairness shows that there is generally a high degree of moral idealism in the occupational aspirations of American teachers (Lortie, 1975, 69).

Teachers who are concerned that they be viewed as fair try to discharge their daily tasks in fair ways. It is through their fairly discharging such discrete tasks as assigning grades to daily assignments and distributing "turns" during discussions and assistance during seatwork periods that they achieve, or fail to achieve, their fairness. The paternalism that liberal egalitarian teachers practice in an effort to bring out the best work from their students is, in other words, one of the ways through which they practice fairness. That fairness is not something they pursue because of personal whim; rather, it is something that they think of as being mandated of them by the ethics of their profession. They imply that fairness is so important in teaching that teachers who ignore it could not satisfactorily remedy their moral neglect by giving compensatory attention to other moral principles. According to their thinking, fairness is the first professional principle among all principles, making the paternalism that they put into their daily work crucial to their competence as fair practitioners.

Paternalistically motivated psychological leadership is just one of the ways liberal egalitarian teachers try to achieve the fairness they see to be incumbent upon themselves. In addition to the paternalism, they believe that they should evaluate completed work according to general quality standards. In short, they think that fairness involves both trying to inspire students to do their best work and then using general standards to determine how good that best work is. These two sides to the practice of fairness in teaching—motivating learning and evaluating assignments—make it necessary for liberal egalitarian teachers to coordinate psychological leadership and evaluation within the same occupational role. The two sides to fairness are not easily reconciled (Lortie, 1975, 151–55).

Teachers employ code words to convey that in practice they must make compromises between the two sides to their role. For example, labels provided by the five teachers for their paternalistic work included "caring" (Hall), "liberal" (Heckman), "easy grader" (Duffy), "going down the road for students" (McGraw), and "egalitarian" (Vackaro). Labels for applying general standards to homework included "being hard" (Hall and Heckman), "not being a spoon-feeder" (Duffy), "not giving gifts" (McGraw), and "concentrating on excellence" (Vackaro). The two categories of labels the teachers use imply that for them the challenge of being fair is essentially the challenge of finding an acceptable balance between being "caring" and being "hard," between "going down the road for students" and "not giving gifts," and so on. Their view is that a fair teacher paternalistically should inspire all members of the class to use their academic endowments and should also inform the members of the class about the quality of their work based on general standards applied to everyone.

Charles Bidwell and Bryan Wilson observe that "advocacy" of individual student involvement and "objective assessment" of the consequences of the involvement are the basics of teaching in modern educational systems and are the cause of much of the role-conflict teachers experience (Bidwell, 1965, 979; Wilson, 1962, 27). Lortie argues that advocacy and assessment often are in conflict for teachers because the "news" they must candidly report back to students sometimes makes it more difficult to sustain the students' continued involvement in studying (Lortie, 1975, 155–59). It might be that having students concentrate on their own work is one way teachers strive to reduce the conflict between their motivation and evaluation duties. Their strategy could be to reduce demoralization caused by class ranking by having the students learn to ignore one another. If such a strategy worked, it would not only be the students who gained by learning more. Since the satisfaction that teachers get from their work is influenced by their own judgments of their effectiveness, a strategy that succeeds by reducing vexing role-conflict helps teachers gain more fulfillment from their occupation than they would otherwise get (Lortie, 1975, 141).

The Discouraging Effect of Social Comparisons

By practicing liberal egalitarian paternalism teachers show that they accept individual students, instead of the students' families and communities, as the "basic unit." The aim of the paternalism is to obtain from students work that is their own and that reflects the natural endowments belonging to them.

Liberal egalitarian teachers regard families and communities as the source of many of the handicaps to learning. Because they consider themselves to be obligated to help students overcome difficulties, they typically view families and communities as competing against them for educational influence. Generally, they want families and communities to support their academic objectives rather than oppose them (Fishkin, 1983, 35–43; Lortie, 1975, 191). For example, if parents tell a child that it is best for him or her to follow along in their footsteps and live as they do, then the child's liberal egalitarian teacher would see the parents as a competitor: The teacher can't assume that the student's academic endowments are suitable only for the kind of work the parents are doing. Suppose that an eight-year-old daughter is talented in math and science, while the mother is a homemaker and the father is a blue-collar worker. If the daughter were to live as they do, she might never exploit her talents. Liberal egalitarian teachers look upon their students as individual persons who stand apart from their families and communities and who have a right to be helped to accomplish, on their own, learning that they do not want to accept because of their families' and communities' values. Such teachers look forward to working with students whose families and communities support academic goals. When the families and communities inhibit rather than support goals, it becomes morally incumbent upon the liberal teacher to provide psychological leadership.

School classrooms are just as much social places as families and communities are. They are places where young people and one adult fill the roles of students and teacher. They fill these roles in relatively close quarters, easily visible to one another. It is therefore easy for students to make social comparisons between achievers on the basis of what they see, even when grades are kept confidential. Everything is so much on display that even the request for a confidential talk ("Susan, please come up to my desk; I would like a quiet talk with you") becomes a public event. Liberal egalitarian fairness challenges teachers to try to help students overcome demoralization caused by their observations of their standing within the class.

For example, imagine that Jim McGraw is teaching an eleventh-grade social studies class. In McGraw's school district, levels one, two, and three students are routinely mixed together in social studies classes; these levels serve as dividers between ability groups. In this eleventh-grade class McGraw has students from all three levels. Imagine that in the fall all of his students were inspired by his leadership to produce their best work. Inevitably, there is much variation in the quality of that work because the ability differences between the students are great. Imagine that it is now February and McGraw's students have gathered a lot of information about where they each stand as an achiever among other achievers. McGraw has not told the students the ranking,

yet they have inferred it from hours of observing each other
answer questions and offer comments. Reflecting upon the way
comparisons happen even when the teacher does not intend them,
McGraw says to you:

> If I were a kid with a reading problem—these kids, they're not
> naive, they know the college kids, they can identify them—and
> if I'm sitting in a room with college prep kids, and I know I
> can't read well or write well, there's just so much intimidation
> that goes on there, unspoken. It's not like the kids walk into a
> room and say, "Hey you dummy, I'm a college prep." It's an
> unspoken thing. The low-level kids can see participation skills.
> The high-level kids can see speaking skills. When I hand back
> papers they know who gets the higher points and who doesn't.

Consider the irony in McGraw's situation. Now, in February, he
is being challenged to cope with an undesirable by-product of his
effective paternalism. Because of his psychological leadership his
students have all risen above the social handicaps they brought
with them into the classroom and have done their best work.
Now, they have no one but themselves to credit, or blame, for
their academic ranking. They cannot point to limitations imposed
upon them by their families and communities; they stand absolutely alone behind their work. Some of McGraw's students are
quite pleased by their position in the class; others are not pleased at
all and are becoming discouraged. To the discouraged it seems
that doing one's best simply confirms an inferiority to others.
Why provide further confirmation, they ask themselves; why not
stop studying and claim that the course is stupid and boring?

Envy and arrogance are present now, in February, in
McGraw's classroom, yet as a liberal egalitarian practitioner he
continues to be obligated to help individual students overcome the
demoralization and laziness induced by their observations. Having been effective at motivating students of varying abilities to do
their best, McGraw now is obligated to help individuals to ignore
the social distinctions that are based upon their best.

Perhaps we can appreciate better now why it is difficult for
McGraw to strike a balance between "going down the road for
students" and "not giving gifts." As a person who believes that all

young students have a right to an education limited only by their personal endowments, McGraw accepts motivating learning as part of being fair to individual right holders. Yet, for the sake of fairness he also candidly tells the students about the quality of their work: From that and other information gained by daily observations, they learn their class ranking. Still, it remains incumbent upon McGraw to cope with the psychological consequences of the students' comparisons: He believes that it would not be fair to the lazy and demoralized students to let them give up.

Why Teachers Prefer That Students Do Their Assignments Alone

Our moral ideals set limits on what we can accept as a permissible solution to a problem. For example, among teachers who have a liberal egalitatian view of their work, it is not permissible to resolve role-conflict by abandoning one or the other of their two duties. If they were to stop their efforts to motivate students, some students who would otherwise stay involved might stop trying. That would not be fair to them. And if teachers were to stop applying general evaluation standards to the students' work, students might develop unrealistic aspirations for their lives after graduation. That would not be fair to them either. However difficult it may be for teachers to incorporate within the same occupational role the motivating and evaluating of all students, according to the liberal egalitarian ideal they are duty-bound to persist in both activities.

The culture of schools stresses that teachers be effective at maintaining control of their classes, but the cooperation of students is by no means automatic (Gordon, 1957, 42; Lortie, 1975, 137). By law youngsters must attend school, and some rebel at the coercion that is part of the student–teacher relationship. Teachers must win the cooperation of young people who may be reluctant to give it, and there are moral and legal limits to the ways the cooperation can be won. For example, teachers cannot use corporal punishment to get the cooperation they need, and they expose themselves to moral criticism if they seek social control at the expense of students' self-respect. Basically, cooperation must be won by offering rewards instead of by imposing penalties, but teachers have few rewards that students want. They can give high marks for "good citizenship," but the students who are most difficult to control often do not care about marks. They can praise, but often students are more concerned about praise from peers than praise from adults in positions of authority. It is ironic that teachers need the cooperation of their students in order to fulfill the basic mandate that they keep control of their classes. Organizationally, teachers are in a supervisory position, but in practice they are dependent upon the groups they are expected to supervise (Bidwell, 1965, 991). This dilemma is behind many of the practices teachers employ to establish and maintain control of their classes. For example, a standard part of teachers' occupational lore is that it is best to start a new school year by rigorously enforcing the rules and then ease up on the rules later. This practice, called "strategic leniency" by the organizational theorists Peter Blau and Marshall Meyer, works by evoking in students a feeling of gratitude that the rules are no longer being rigorously applied although they could be (Blau & Meyer, 1971, 63). In return, the students provide basic cooperation to the teacher as an incentive for not returning to the harsh measures that characterized the beginning of the year (Waller, n.d., 292–317).

Teachers are not inclined to approve of any new approach to teaching that they judge may make controlling students even more difficult than it already is. Some may fear that if they were to depart from the routine of having students work alone on their homework, it would be even more difficult to keep control of them. Those teachers may think that in order to conquer students, they must keep them divided. Teachers who think along these lines would conclude that student collaboration is impractical.

I developed the point not long ago that the liberal egalitarian ideal prescribes that teachers help their students overcome social deprivation so that they can apply all of their natural endowments to doing their best work. I also observed that the rankings that emerge as students of varied endowments do their best become a kind of social deprivation that teachers must help students overcome in order that they may continue with their studies. Teaching students of varied ability in the same classroom entails not only the difficulty of selecting material that challenges the best students while not overwhelming the worst, but also the difficulty of maintaining every student's motivation to do his or her best, despite the fact that it results in inequality with others. When the well endowed do their best, they rise to the top of the class. They well might wonder why they should continue to work their hardest when they can produce acceptable work by not working very hard. And the poorly endowed might wonder why they should keep doing their best when doing so puts them in an inferior social postition, which they perceive themselves as deserving because they "earned" it on their own (Schaar, 1967, 235). Teachers must find some way to make comprehensible to students that although they are all equal as persons, they are unequal in their qualifications; moreover, teachers must convey this perspective in a way that encourages neither envy among the poorly endowed nor arrogance among the well endowed.

It may be that one way teachers try to reconcile the conflicting claims of equality and inequality is by having students work alone. They may reason that this approach makes it less likely that students will notice and be bothered by differences among them as achievers. Having students remain at their own desks and focused on their own seatwork would be like putting blinders on a horse. With their "blinders" on, students have no alternative but to look straight ahead at their own work, and their morale will not be jeopardized by social comparisons. Also, the directive that students work alone seems to be consistent with the liberals' conviction that individual persons are the "basic unit" of life. In a society where the individual, not the group, is regarded as basic, it is not surprising the teachers expect their approaches to reflect the priority that society gives to individuals, and they may believe that having students work alone is one way to do that.

Concluding Remarks

There are many reasons why teachers think the way they do, and they do not all think the same way. Teachers are influenced by tradition. The socialization provided by their teacher education provides them with additional vocabulary and perspective.

Afterwards, on the job, their thinking is influenced by organizational constraints and professional associations. However, behind all these factors stands American culture with its enduring emphasis upon individuality and the importance of learning how to provide for oneself. Not surprisingly, teachers' thinking resonates with basic, culturally legitimated views about persons as moral subjects.

In the preceding pages, I used the thinking of five teachers to illustrate the expression of a liberal egalitarian philosophy of education by practitioners who probably never had the opportunity to study the philosophy formally. I have no reliable generalizations to offer concerning the percentage of teachers in the United states who think in a basically liberal egalitarian manner, nor am I prepared to identify precisely the boundaries between liberal egalitarian thinking and other ways of understanding one's basic mission as a teacher. That would be difficult to do. However, the experience of teaching courses in the philosophy of education to teachers for 17 years has given me the impression that many teachers would agree that fairness to individual students is a basic professional mandate and that fairness involves reducing any impediments provided by society so that students may use fully whatever endowments they have. Moreover, I have the impression that many teachers would agree that endowments belong normatively to individual persons, not, as Rawls recommends, to everyone together as ingredients of a collectively owned pool. In summary, I believe, but cannot prove, that the thinking that I have analyzed in this chapter is to a large extent the thinking of many American teachers about their professional responsibilities. As for the five teachers whom I have discussed in this chapter, all of them have had the opportunity to evaluate my analysis of their thinking. Two teachers took advantage of the opportunity to evaluate, and their evaluations are reported in Appendix B.

I don't know for certain that teachers believe that they reduce the operational conflict between student equality and inequality in academic achievement by having students work alone. I am speculating that some teachers may think this way. I am speculating that some consider that working alone is one way to make evident the liberal theorists' assertion about the worth of students as individual persons. In the next chapter I shall use liberal principles to show why such a plausibly liberal endorsement of a routine of studying independently is wrong. It is wrong, I shall argue, for teachers to hold that they must have students work alone in order to demonstrate that individual persons are, to use Daniel Bell's words, the "basic units" of life.

CHAPTER 3

The Social Nature
of Academic Achievement

I have speculated that there is a connection between the practice in our nation's schools of having students work alone and the ideal of equal opportunity as it is understood by liberal egalitarians. Behind that ideal is a conception of a person as a moral subject, according to which all persons are equally protected and are not to be disadvantaged by social attributes when they are young because the attributes do not belong to them as individuals. A student's rank in a classroom is one such attribute, and therefore in fairness it should not be permitted to impede a student's learning. Moreover, if studying alone helps students pay attention only to their work and thereby helps them ignore their ranking, then studying alone is desirable. The fairness is confirmed when all students do their best work, that is, work that reflects their natural endowments and nothing else.

In this chapter I shall present the liberal egalitarian criticism of the thinking I just reviewed, thinking that educators might accept as faithful to the ideal of fairness to everyone in a liberal egalitarian way. Because I will be using liberal egalitarian principles to argue against one application of those principles to teaching, it may seem to some readers as if I am turning the morality against itself. My maneuvering will not, I hope, cause the morality to devour itself, so that nothing will be left behind to suggest to future generations that there was once alive a view of fairness in education that called for full utilization of one's natural endowments without hinderance by society. My goal is to give new impetus to the liberal egalitarian vision of fair education, an impetus that accommodates both the realities of classroom life and a moral conception of a person as a protected individual whose self-understanding includes a commitment to friendship and generosity toward others.

The Self-Understanding Needed for Autonomy

The overriding goal of liberal egalitarian teaching is to promote personal autonomy among students so that as adults they will be able to live their own lives. Because autonomy depends, in part, upon knowledge, one way in which teaching promotes autonomy is by helping students do their best academically. The more people know, the better prepared they are to choose suitable plans for themselves and to find the best means for accomplishing their plans. The goal of liberal egalitarian teaching is to help transform immature persons into mature adults who live their *own* lives as self-determining agents. However, the ability to live one's own life as a self-determining adult involves more than the accumulation of academic knowledge. It also requires that people become proficient at differentiating between themselves as agents and the alternative ways of life presented for their approval. In the following paragraphs I will bring out the nature of these differentiations.

The lives of self-determining persons have patterns. Consider, for example, Julie's mother, Professor Gates. Certain things repeat daily in her life: She goes to her office at the university in the morning, prepares for her classes, teaches, continues with her research, and attends committee meetings. This pattern would lead an observer to conclude that Gates is getting things done. But infants have patterns to their lives too. When she was a baby, Julie got hungry at about the same times every day; she expected her mother to walk through the front door at about the same time every afternoon; and she got sleepy at about the same time after supper. Furthermore, nonliving things act in patterned ways. The geyser Old Faithful has been erupting hourly for years and attracting visitors to its show. What is it that makes the patterned behavior of self-determining agents different from other patterns such as those of the geyser's eruptions?

The philosopher Charles Taylor brings out what is special to the patterns of self-determining agents by calling attention to the fact that while patterns can be described in a variety of ways, for self-determining agents one of the pattern descriptions will be more "privileged" than the others (Taylor, 1985b, 260). Consider what I am doing this very moment. One observer might say that I am writing a book. A second observer might conclude that I am earning a living. And a third observer might claim that I am using up ink and paper. Now consider the geyser. One tourist might say that Old Faithful is releasing underground pressure. Another tourist might reply that the geyser is amusing the tourists. And a third tourist might add, "Old Faithful is increasing Wyoming's revenues." In the case of the geyser, all of the pattern descriptions would be equally privileged, but in my case the description of me as engaged in writing a book would be more "privileged" than the others.

But why is a privilege operating in my case and not in the geyser's? In my case the pattern is to an action in pursuit of an end, but in the geyser's case there is no reason to think that there is an end being pursued. However, nonliving things can pursue ends too, so the agency of self-determining persons is not distinguished from that of nonliving things simply by the pursuit of an end. It is necessary to consider the nature of the end being pursued.

As a way of bringing out the difference between pursuing a chosen end and pursuing an end given to the pursuer by someone else, Taylor asks us to think of self-guided missiles (Taylor, 1985b, 258). Missiles are equipped with a mechanism that processes information through a feedback control so that they will remain directed toward their target. The pattern to a missile's flight has a purpose, just as the pattern to my actions right now has a purpose. But in the case of a missile, the purpose is not one that the missile chose for itself: The missile was programmed by engineers for the purpose of striking a target. On the other hand, I chose to spend my time today writing about the purposes of self-determining persons. I approved of my purpose for myself; the purpose was not given to me by engineers. That is why the description of me as writing about purposes is privileged above the competing pattern descriptions of me as earning a living or using up ink and paper. It is my view of what I am doing that gives privilege to the pattern description of me as writing.

The self-understanding of an autonomous person is grounded upon differentiations made by that person and no one else. Other people cannot grasp for that person the insight that an agent-evaluator of alternative purposes and the purposes themselves are not the same. Thus, for the writing I am doing to be my writing, I must apprehend for myself that I as an agent and the writing I am doing are different. If I were to see them as the same, I would be so immersed in the writing that I could not grasp that I, as an agent of action, could have chosen to use my time to do something other than write (Sandel, 1982, 56).

The ability to differentiate between oneself as an agent and competing purposes is what immature persons lack, and so long as they lack it they cannot live their own lives. They cannot become connected by possession to the lives they are living—they cannot become engaged in living their *own* lives—until they are able to see reflexively that as agents they are distanced from the lives they are living, just as actors stand at a distance from the roles they play. People are self-determining only when they grasp that they and the lives they are living are different. The freedom provided by their appreciation of the difference is reflected in their approval or disapproval of the way they are living.

Professor Gates is living the life of a philosopher. It is her own life because she approves of it (she thinks of herself as able to pursue some other life, but this is the one she prefers). Occasionally Gates becomes so absorbed in her career that it ceases to be part of her own life because she has lost her perspective and no longer differentiates between herself and the career. Losing her perspective, she also loses her freedom, and when this happens, her friends begin to worry about her out of concern that in this state she will both wear herself out and neglect her other responsibilities. They share with her their perceptions of what has happened to her and try their best to help her regain the perspective that she as an agent and the career she is pursuing are not one and the same. They want to help her regain her perspective so that she can take charge of her living again. Once Gates regains the ability to differentiate between herself as an agent and the career she is pursuing, she can work for balance between the time she puts into the career and the time she gives to the other things she has taken on, such as being a parent to Julie.

Education That Helps Youth Develop Their Own Agency

Training cannot lead to an ability to live one's own life because training only produces conditioned habits of response that are automatically triggered by stimuli. A child can be trained to place her hand over her mouth when she coughs; later, she can be trained by her kindergarten teacher to proceed immediately to her assigned seat when she enters the classroom. But she is not living her own life as she places her hand over her mouth and as she heads toward her seat. As a product of training, she has no apprehension that she is an agent who could be doing otherwise.

Liberal egalitarians maintain that education should be more than training and that the overriding objective of education is to help people become able to live their own lives as self-determining agents. They maintain that becoming free to live one's own life is a worthy goal in itself because doing so characterizes being fully human. Thus, from their point of view, becoming educated is not merely a means to some other valuable end, in the way that, for example, a visit to a doctor's office is a means to shaking the flu, or paying the price of a ticket is a means to admission to a concert. The worth of education is not merely dependent on the things educated persons do. It is also dependent on the perspective they have toward what they do: They apprehend that they are persons who could be doing otherwise yet do what they do because they approve of it. This perspective makes them free.

Liberal egalitarians view persons morally as protected individuals, and empirically as culturally and socially situated. They maintain that people become autonomous by learning how to look upon themselves as agents who are situated in a society but who are not constituted by their situation. When people learn how to look upon themselves this way they become able to approve or disapprove of their situations and to work for situations that fit a coherent life plan they have chosen for themselves. Young people cannot become agents so long as the social attributes of their lives remain invisible to them. So long as they confusedly accept as constituents of themselves what are in reality their social attributes, they will not be able to differentiate between themselves and the attributes. Thus, liberal egalitarian teachers who value autonomy must help students learn how to recognize the social attributes of their lives for what they are. The attributes should be looked upon as objects to be evaluated by individuals, not to be blindly accepted because of the interpretation that, whatever they may be for any particular individual, they must always be constitutively present in that individual.

Frequently we speak of the knowledge a person has, but do we mean the knowledge that physically *goes with* the person or the knowledge that *belongs* to the person normatively? For the academic knowledge that students gain to be their knowledge normatively, they must be helped by their teachers to see the social nature of the knowledge. Otherwise, they will not be able to differentiate between themselves as agents and the knowledge they have as physical beings. Without that differentiation, the knowledge cannot belong to them normatively. Knowledge becomes theirs only when they give their approval to it, and that approval must rest upon their realization that the knowledge is arbitrary to them as individual agents, however useful it may be to them.

Imagine that Julie is studying Spanish under Jim Hall, chemistry under Jan Heckman, and history under Jim McGraw. From this studying, Julie comes to know all kinds of things. For example, she comes to know that in Spanish the word *bellaco* means "scoundrel." This bit of vocabulary becomes part of her knowledge of Spanish. For Julie's knowledge of Spanish to be not only knowledge that she has physically but also knowledge that belongs to her normatively, she must be free to approve of the knowledge for herself. She must be personally committed to the knowledge. For Julie to provide the commitment, she must acquire some knowledge of the social nature of the knowledge of Spanish that she has physically.

The knowledge Julie is gaining from overt instruction can be thought of as first-level knowledge: Seeing the connection between *bellaco* and "scoundrel" is part of her first-level knowledge. Any knowledge about the social nature of her first-level knowledge would constitute a kind of second-level knowledge: Second-level knowledge is knowledge about knowledge. Julie's teachers must help her to reach a second-level knowledge in order for the academic knowledge she is gaining to become relevant to her freedom. But is it prudent to recommend that teachers take on the additional responsibility of promoting insight into the social nature of academic knowledge? After all, teachers have their hands full controlling their classes and helping individual students achieve the first-level academic knowledge needed to pass tests and to qualify for more advanced courses. Is it reasonable to saddle teachers with another responsibility when they already regard themselves as overbooked?

My answer to the above questions is that it is not necessary for teachers deliberately to convey second-level knowledge in the way they teach subjects like Spanish, chemistry, and history. If teachers exploit the hidden curriculum properly, they can teach "between the lines" in a way that makes apparent to students like Julie that the knowledge they are gaining has a social basis. However, the evidence is that today students are not being exposed to a hidden curriculum that invites such insight into the social nature of knowledge. And without the insight, the knowledge they are gaining will not be relevant to their autonomy.

Miseducation Caused by the Routine of Studying Alone

We have noted that John Goodlad's observers found that youngsters in our nation's classrooms usually work alone. To illustrate how the experience of routinely working alone affects students' perspective on their own knowledge, imagine that Julie is now an eleventh grader: All her life as a student she has had dedicated teachers who inspired her to apply her academic talents to her work; she has achieved a good record and is well liked by both her teachers and fellow students. Julie has matured enough to understand that in her classes she and her classmates are performing a role that they leave behind when they walk away from the school and into the community. She understands that she, Julie the person, is not the same as the role that she performs in the classroom, and she can contrast the way her present teachers interpret the role of student with the way her former teachers interpreted it.

However, when Julie refers to the knowledge that she gains from her studying as "her" knowledge, she simply means that she now bears the knowledge. She views herself as having earned the knowledge by working for it, and now the knowledge is "hers" in the sense that when people ask for evidence of what she knows, she can show them. But Julie is not yet able to detach herself critically from the knowledge she now bears, because she does not see the social nature of the knowledge. Indeed, she thinks of the knowledge as something that is "inside" her head, making it private and personal, not social. The hidden curriculum provided by the routine of working alone for knowledge has led Julie to regard what has happened to her this way. Unfortunately, she is mistaken.

The Intrinsically Social Nature of Knowledge

Julie's perspective on her achievements is not unusual. Many people think of themselves as having minds into which they put information and knowledge: They think of their minds as being private, not public, and personal, not social. However, the philosopher Ludwig Wittgenstein shows that knowledge is not private and personal in the sense that, in principle, it might forever remain inside a person's mind, inaccessible to others. Wittgenstein brings out the social nature of knowledge by analyzing what is involved in following a rule. In the following paragraphs I will review the philosopher Peter Winch's account, in *The Idea of a Social Science and Its Relation to Philosophy* (1958), of Wittgenstein's analysis.

Jim Hall has been teaching Julie that *bellaco* means "scoundrel." Today Hall reads Julie's test to determine whether or not she has learned the meaning of the new vocabulary words. One of Hall's concerns is that Julie know the definition of *bellaco*.

When people know a definition, they use the word in the same way each time they use it. But what is involved in using a word like *bellaco* in the *same* way? How is it possible for Hall to decide whether or not Julie's use of *bellaco* is the same as or different from the use dictated by the definition of the word? Following Wittgenstein, Winch explains, "It is only in terms of a given *rule* that we can attach a specific sense to the words 'the same'" (Winch,

1958, 29). People are able to use words in the same way by following rules. But what is involved in following rules?

Winch brings out what Wittgenstein means by "following" a rule by asking us to imagine a person, A, who is writing down the figures 1 3 5 7 on a blackboard. A asks his friend, B, how the series is to be continued.

> Almost everybody in this situation, short of having special reasons to be suspicious, would answer: 9 11 13 15. Let us suppose that A refuses to accept this as a continuation of his series, saying it runs as follows: 1 3 5 7 1 3 5 7 9 11 13 15 9 11 13 15. He then asks B to continue from there. At this point B has a variety of alternatives to choose from. Let us suppose that he makes a choice and that A again refuses to accept it, but substitutes another continuation of his own. And let us suppose that this continues for some time. There would undoubtedly come a point at which B, with perfect justification, would say that A was not really following a mathematical rule at all, even though all the continuations he had made to date *could* be brought within the scope of some formula. Certainly A was following a rule; but his rule was: Always to substitute a continuation different from the one suggested by B at every stage. And though this is a perfectly good rule of its kind, it does not belong to arithmetic. (Winch, 1958, 29–30)

B's justified reaction that A is not following a mathematical rule suggests an important feature of the concept of following a rule. That is, we must take account of not only the actions of the person who is allegedly following the rule but the reactions of other people as well to what the person is doing. People can be said to follow rules only when in truth there is a rule to be discovered by analysis of their behavior. Thus, when persons follow rules, they risk making a mistake that can be detected by others.

> A mistake is a contravention of what is *established* as correct; as such, it must be *recognisable* as such a contravention. That is, if I make a mistake in, say, my use of a word, other people must be able to point it out to me. If this is not so, I can do what I like and there is no external check on what I do; that is, nothing is established. Establishing a standard is not an activity which it

makes sense to ascribe to any individual in complete isolation from other individuals. For it is contact with other individuals which alone makes possible the external check on one's actions which is inseparable from an established standard. (Winch, 1958, 32)

Helped by Wittgenstein, Winch points out that when people maintain that they know something in principle, they are at risk of making a mistake. For any statement to be a mistake, it must be recognizable to other persons as a violation of a standard or rule that they follow together as members of a community.

Like Wittgenstein, I maintain that no person can attain an entirely personal, private knowledge of anything that must remain inaccessible to others. When Julie achieves an understanding of a Spanish word, or of anything else, she then inhabits a community of persons who all follow the same rules that provide the grounding for the understanding. The hidden curriculum that Julie is exposed to should help her see that everything she is learning in order to pass her tests and complete her assignments is grounded upon rules that are collectively followed, in this case, by all speakers of Spanish. Julie will become able to give her approval to her knowledge of a subject only if she develops an understanding of herself as an agent who stands behind the knowledge that she has physically. To develop that understanding, she must be helped to see the social grounding of her knowledge.

Even after Julie has mastered the meaning of *bellaco,* she still does not own the linguistic rule on the basis of which *bellaco* means "scoundrel." That rule does not and never will belong to her in the sense that she will have a right of first use of the rule and therefore may deny anyone else use of it if she wishes. This is true of all the knowledge that students gain from being taught and from doing their assignments: All academic knowledge is grounded upon inhabiting a community of persons who use the same rules together. All academic courses offered are language courses in the sense that they all teach students how to follow linguistic rules on the basis of which mistakes can be identified. Of course, what constitutes a mistake in a Spanish course is not the same as what constitutes a mistake in a chemistry or history course. The rules upon which the various academic subjects are grounded vary in the degree of their precision. A mistaken solution to a quadratic equation can be more confidently identified by authorities than mistaken interpretations of poems and paintings. Nevertheless, what students learn from their courses might in principle be shareable with others, and that sharing consists of their collective inhabitation of the same linguistic communities.

Learning a language, whether it is Spanish, algebra, or literary criticism, is a process of being initiated into a community of other language users.[1] Charles Taylor explains:

> . . . now a language, and the related set of distinctions underlying our experience and interpretation, is something that can only grow in and be sustained by a community. In that sense, what we are as human beings, we are only in a cultural community. Perhaps, once we have fully grown up in a culture, we can leave it and still retain much of it. But this kind of case is exceptional, and in an important sense marginal. Emigrés cannot fully leave their culture, and are always forced to take on something of the ways of the new society they have entered. The life of a language and culture is one whose locus is larger than that of the individual. It happens in the community. The individual possesses this culture, and hence his identity, by participating in this larger life. (Taylor, 1984, 182)

When educators plan their curricula, actually they are selecting the communities into which students will be initiated. Wittgenstein explains that communities consist of persons who practice together the same "forms of life." Forms of life are the linguistic, social, and cultural constructions on the basis of which individual persons may belong to the same people (Winch, 1958, 40–42).

Curriculum planning always has implications for civic education because it always involves choosing the communities into which students will be initiated by the instruction provided to them. Thus, when Julie learns the meaning of *bellaco*, she takes one more step in her induction into the community of speakers of Spanish. Formerly, she was an outsider to the community; now, she is gradually becoming an insider. If she becomes fluent, the unique language resources of that community may make it possible for her to have new inner experiences that would otherwise have remained foreign to her.

I observed earlier that enabling students to live as an educated persons is the ultimate aim of liberal egalitarian teaching. Educated persons live their own lives, which they as agents have endorsed for themselves because they have become able to differentiate between themselves as agents and the forms of life into which they have been initiated by their education. They grasp that as individuated agents they stand morally separate from each other but equal to one another. Also, they grasp that they are in partnership with others who practice the same forms of life. They are not all equal in that partnership because in fact some are better at following the rules than others. However, in their partnership they are able to overcome their separation from each other by communicating their knowledge. These are the two conditions of their humanity: Morally, they are individuated from each other, but they are also joined together by the rules that provide coherence to their discourse. Once people understand the social nature of their knowledge, they have reason to be grateful to others because without others there would be no knowledge at all.

The Negative Effect on Autonomy of Studying Alone

It might seem paradoxical that routinely having students do their assignments alone inhibits the development of their autonomy, but that is what I am arguing. People's autonomy is not proven by the fact that they work alone. A slave could be ordered to lay a fire and then left to do the job alone. Julie's mother could exercise her autonomy by consulting with her colleagues on a difficult philosophical problem. Autonomy is not made by what one is doing, solitarily or cooperatively, but by the perspective one has upon what one is doing. Autonomous persons regard what they are doing as *their* action. They claim that the action belongs to them, that they are not acting as an executive of another person's will. They take on responsibility for what they are doing by holding that the actions are *their* actions.

The hidden curriculum in the classrooms visited by John Goodlad's team of observers is giving students false clues about the nature of knowledge and, by doing so, is delaying the development of their autonomy. The curriculum is camouflaging the nature of knowledge by making knowledge look like it is a private, personal phenomenon. The question of whether or not they approve of the knowledge they are gaining never occurs to students because they do not see that they as agents and the knowledge they have gained are not the same. They begin to think of themselves as persons who are constituted by the knowledge they have. This thinking makes it more difficult for them to understand that they are all morally equal. After all, some know more than others, and if it is true that we are constituted by what we know, then it is also true that we are unequal. In this frame of mind, students are not only less likely to discover that they as persons can stand at a distance from the knowledge they have gained; they are also less likely to keep their self-respect when they discover that they know less than others. The self that deserves to be respected is so tightly connected to the knowledge had by the self that it is diminished by the lack of knowledge.

Teachers who are devoted to liberal egalitarian ideals should provide a hidden curriculum that makes as plausible as possible for students the insight that knowledge is socially grounded. One way to provide the plausibility is to have students periodically collaborate with each other, that is, talk about a subject together; as students talk, they would observe one another trying to follow the same rules. The collaboration would make visible to the participants their partnership in the same community of rule followers, and this visibility would convey to them the idea that knowledge is social in nature. Grasping that idea would move students closer to the autonomy that liberal egalitarians seek for everyone, because the students would be able to differentiate between themselves and their knowledge.

I am not arguing that students should always collaborate and never work alone. Such a radical shift in approach would create new kinds of false clues just as misleading as those now being provided by the routine of studying alone. There are no panaceas to the problem of improving the quality of education for our nation's youth. While I maintain that periodic collaboration in classrooms would help students achieve the kind of self-understanding and autonomy that are consistent with the liberal conception of a person, this is not the only thing that needs to be done to improve education. Collaborative studying should be just one of several methods used by teachers, and students should continue to have opportunities to do some of their work independently in order that they might gain further insight into the extent and distribution of their intellectual powers. I am not denying that solitary studying can be a source of immense satisfaction and insight. I am simply maintaining that studying alone all the time gives students a distorted view of what learning is. Educators need to be attentive not only to what they tell students about learning but also to what they convey to students about the nature of learning by the ways in which they permit students to treat each other in the process.

One might ask why some students are able to rebel against the instruction they are receiving even though they are not able to differentiate between themselves and their knowledge. Isn't their rebellion evidence that they have discovered that they are agents? However, if my criticism of the hidden curriculum is valid, the routine of solitary studying would have prevented them from discovering that they and the knowledge they have gained become normatively connected by individual approval. So, how is their rebellion to be explained?

There are many explanations for student rebellion because there are many causes of it. Some of the causes lie outside the classroom, in families and communities. Others are developmental: Youngsters challenge adults as part of the process of growing up. But it is not knowledge itself against which they rebel. Rather, it is the social relationships they are put into as they learn in classrooms that offend them and that they therefore rebel against. To repeat, classroom life is social life; it is a life of working among other students, all of whom are subordinate to the teacher. When students say "I don't like math," it is not mathematical knowledge itself that they disapprove of, but instead the social relationships they experience as they are challenged to acquire the knowledge. For example, how can Julie like math if she discovers that as a math student she consistently ranks among the worst students in the class? It is not the subject that she dislikes; rather, it is the social relationship she is in *vis à vis* her teacher and classmates that she objects to. It is seldom pleasing to be among the worst at something.

On the other hand, collaborative studying might give those who are having trouble with a subject a reason to value their more able classmates. They might appreciate the fact that by collaborating with their more talented classmates they can do better at the subject than they could do otherwise. The position of being one of the worst performers never will be ideal, but it might be less loathsome if the worst performers see that they are advantaged by having more talented persons around them. Sometimes we find ourselves in exactly this position outside of classrooms. When we go to a concert or the theater, we find ourselves being inspired by performers who are much more accomplished at their art than we could ever be. And this is not just because we have never applied ourselves to mastering the art. I have been a student of the piano for many years. Because I have applied myself to do as well as I can and have learned how limited my talent for music is, I find the performance of a great pianist especially inspiring. I am grateful for such talent, not envious of it. Why can't less talented students be helped to be grateful for those around them who are more talented? And wouldn't they be more likely to be grateful if they could get some help?

Some Empirical Research on Collaborative Learning

Research comparing the effect on learning of collaborating with others, competing against others, and working independently has been done in laboratories, industrial settings, and schools.[2] In schools, researchers have investigated the effect of collaboration on academic achievement and student attitudes. By convention they speak of the attitudes of persons as the ingredients of their "social connectedness"; included in social connectedness are interpersonal attraction, friendliness, positive group evaluation, and helpfulness. Researchers find that when students collaborate on academics, they show greater gains in their social connectedness than when they compete against each other or work independently (Slavin, 1977, 644–45). In general, research shows that when students work collaboratively, they grow to like each other more. This finding should be of interest to teachers who are being challenged to improve interpersonal acceptance between students in multiracial and multiethnic classrooms. However, not all classrooms have a multiracial or multiethnic composition, but teachers in all classrooms view individual academic achievement as the basic aim of teaching. Teachers cannot accept a better way of increasing interpersonal acceptance if that way produces lower academic achievement than is produced by either competitive or independent ways of doing schoolwork.

Unfortunately, researchers for a long time have had difficulty proving that collaboration consistently produces higher academic achievement for all students than the other two approaches produce. Recently, however, Robert Slavin has had some success at explaining why experiments in collaborative studying have not consistently shown superior gains for all students. Slavin finds that inconsistent results arise from differences in the kinds of assignments students were given (Slavin, 1983, 11–13). For example, in one study four students were each given three unique numbers between one and thirteen and were asked to find the missing number. Because of the nature of the assignment, the students could more quickly find the missing number by working cooperatively than by working alone (Slavin, 1983, 54). Slavin explains that this assignment is similar to many others that researchers have given students, in that they are by nature more suitable for collaborative problem solving than for one of the other two methods. Slavin concludes that comparisons between research studies should take into account the kind of assignment given to participants, so that assignments that are suitable for cooperation will not be mixed with assignments that are not inherently suitable. Moreover, he predicts that cooperative learning will not be widely accepted in schools until researchers figure out how assignments that are not inherently suitable for cooperation can consistently lead to higher achievement for all students.

Still another problem researchers must solve is the one of lazy students who are glad to have others do their work when they are given the opportunity to collaborate. Slavin has been particularly interested in devising ways of organizing collaboration so that individual students will have an incentive to work. The problem, he says, is that some assignments have been organized in a way that diffuses responsibility, and when diffusion occurs some students are left free to let others do all the work, without jeopardizing the success of the entire group (Slavin, 1983, 14). Slavin believes that diffusion of responsibility while studying for a group reward can be prevented by making individual contributions so visible to others that teammates can distinguish easily between contributing and noncontributing members: "This may be done by making the group reward depend upon the sum of the members' performances (as in wrestling or a chess team), or by giving each member a unique subtask (as in an assembly line)" (Slavin, 1983, 16).

Slavin has extensively tested several academic games that make individual results obvious to all the members of a team and, by doing so, give every member an incentive to try hard. He reports that when the specific duties of individual teammates are made clear to everyone on a team so that everyone can see how well each teammate completes his or her job, individual members learn more than they can by working competitively or independently. Three of Slavin's games have been widely used by teachers throughout the country: Student Teams–Achievement Divisions (STAD); Teams–Games–Tournament (TGT); and Jigsaw II (Slavin, 1983, 23–30). Each of the games includes a rule that makes it clear to all teammates what every member contributes to the team score. For example, the STAD game requires that students be divided into four- or five-member learning teams. Each team is to be a microcosm of the ethnic and ability diversity of the entire class. Each week the teacher introduces new material through a lecture or discussion. The team members then study work sheets on the new material. First, they work in pairs by quizzing each other; later, they discuss their problems as a group. They have the answer sheets so that it is clear to them that they are being asked to master concepts instead of memorize a series of answers. Following the team practice, students individually take quizzes on the material. Individual scores are combined into team scores by the teacher. The amount each student contributes to the team score is based upon the degree to which the quiz score exceeds the student's past quiz average. This criterion makes it possible for students to contribute maximum points to a team only if they do their best and improve beyond their past performance. In effect, they each compete against their own past records.

The Ideal Motive for Student Collaborators

Slavin's goals for collaborative studying are not the same as the goals of interest to me. My argument is that periodic collaboration would help make students aware of the social nature of academic achievement and by doing so would help their autonomy, because autonomy involves differentiating between oneself and everything that is social. I am arguing that until students grasp that knowledge is socially grounded, they cannot be responsible for knowledge. It cannot be *their* knowledge until they approve of it, and they cannot approve of it until they see that they and the knowledge are not the same. Collaboration would help students achieve an understanding of what knowledge is, and the autonomy made possible by that insight is a major goal of liberal egalitarian education.

Slavin is interested in maximizing first-level, subject matter knowledge, not in eliciting second-level insight into the nature of knowledge itself. Slavin says that he has found ways to help individual students learn more science, history, and mathematics by cooperating among themselves, but he has not given any attention to the ways in which his games affect the self-understanding of students as persons who are achieving knowledge. So, it is fitting to question whether liberal egalitarians should endorse the use of Slavin's games for goals that lie beyond his goals. Can Slavin's games enhance first-level, subject matter knowledge and also elicit some philosophical insight into the nature of that knowledge? Those who seek philosophical insight for students might be concerned that students who play Slavin's games are told that by helping their teammates they increase their chances of being on a victorious team. Although being on a victorious team may not be their only motive for playing the game, it is one of their motives. The concern is that a preoccupation with victory may not be compatible with the philosophical insight about knowledge that interests me.

I take up this problem in the next chapter. Using liberal egalitarian ideas, I shall examine four different motives for collaboration among students. Two of them will be motives to fulfill a duty; the third will be the motive to do some good; and the fourth will be the motive to be generous to someone. I shall show that generosity is the ideal liberal egalitarian motive and explain why students might have this motive and also the motive to be on the winning team. I conclude that the incentives provided by collaboration-based games need not be an impediment to insight into the social nature of knowledge.

CHAPTER 4

Freedom, Equality, and Generosity

Imagine that we observe Julie and her classmate Pam quizzing each other on their Spanish vocabulary assignment. Obviously, their intention is to help each other do better on the test that is coming up. But, from a liberal egalitarian point of view, what would be the ideal motive for their trying to help each other do better on the test? Below are four different motives that the girls could have for helping each other.

1. *The motive to fulfill a general duty.*
    Julie is the better Spanish student. Her motive in helping Pam is to satisfy the general duty applicable to people everywhere that more talented persons should help less talented ones.
2. *The motive to maximize academic achievement as a basic good.*
    Julie wants her entire class to do as well as possible. She is helping Pam in order to boost the class average on the test. She wants to be part of a "good" Spanish class.
3. *The motive to fulfill a specific duty.*
    Pam helped Julie in chemistry class, and Julie promised Pam that she would help her in return by reviewing with her the Spanish vocabulary. Now, Julie's motive is to fulfill the specific duty she has to Pam.
4. *The motive of being generous to Pam.*
    Julie's motive is to make Pam better off because she cares for her.

In the first and third examples Julie's motives are to do what she believes she ought to do. In the first, it is the motive to fulfill a

57

duty that applies generally to everyone. In the third, it is to fulfill a duty that Julie has to Pam only. On the other hand, in the second example Julie's motive is utilitarian in the sense that she wants to maximize a good, that is, the amount of knowledge had by her entire class. Finally, in the fourth example Julie has generosity as her motive. Here she helps Pam neither because she has a duty to do so nor because doing so will produce more good. Instead, she wants to make Pam, the person, better off by helping Pam increase her knowledge. This motive marks her as being generous to Pam.

John Rawls theorizes that there is a general duty whereby more talented persons should help less talented ones. If Julie's motive for collaborating with Pam were to fulfill that general duty, Rawls could provide her with a theory for that duty. I shall argue, however, that Rawls' general duty theory is unacceptable because it endangers the right to individual liberty that liberals, including Rawls himself, hold to be basic. Next, I shall show that the utilitarian motive to do good is also unacceptable because doing good can violate human equality, another basic liberal value. The motive of generosity, on the other hand, can comply with both liberal requirements of freedom and equality.

John Rawls' General Duty Theory

Rawls explains that his theory of justice implies "an agreement to regard the distribution of natural talent as a common asset and to share in the benefits of this distribution whatever it turns out to be" (Rawls, 1973, 101). His contention is that in behalf of justice people should commit themselves to treating human endowments as ingredients of a common endowment pool. Everyone would have a right to draw from the pool, and drawings would occur in such a way that the lesser endowed become better off than they would become if they worked independently or competitively. This is Rawls' "democratic egalitarian" morality of collective possession, which rivals the liberal egalitarian view that endowments are normatively attached to the individuals who carry them physically.

Rawls is concerned that our exploitation of human endowments be done in a way that ensures everyone a fair share of basic goods. Of course, it is not possible to divide endowments among people in the same way that, say, a strawberry dessert could be divided. If Julie has an excess of mathematical talent and her friend Pam has an excess of musical talent, no physical redistribution could make Julie more musical and Pam a better mathematician. The philosopher Anthony Kronman has considered the way Rawls could achieve a fair distribution of something that cannot be physically divided. Kronman proposes that when Rawls speaks of talents as "communal assets" he does "not mean that the talent itself must somehow be carved up into portions" and distributed to everyone in the community. Rather, he means that a community member "must be prohibited from exploiting the gifts in a way that does not benefit others equally—that he must be prohibited, in other words, from selfishly using his own talent to make himself better off than his neighbors" (Kronman, 1981, 65). Rawls is proposing that well-endowed persons be prohibited from using those endowments in ways that do not benefit others, unless there is some sort of compensation made to others. That compensation would involve service to the less well off. Kronman's interpretation is that talent pooling "represents nothing more than a system of taxation" upon individual endowments in a way that achieves fairness for everyone. As a system of taxation, fairness for everyone might be conceived of as equalizing "the cost to every individual of achieving some specified ends" (Kronman, 1981, 66). The ends would have to be specified, because some people might choose ends that were so ambitious that they would monopolize the entire pool and leave nothing for others. What if Julie, for example, were to decide that she wanted to become a concert pianist? With the limited musical talent she has naturally, she would need the full attention of Pam and every other musically talented person in her class in order to progress toward her ambitious goal. Then, none of the other classmates would be able to get help from the musically talented persons because Julie would be monopolizing all the help.

Kronman theorizes that the ends in light of which the extent of compensatory exchanges are determined should be "minimal ends" that "are likely to be prerequisites for the fulfillment of almost any plan of life" (Kronman, 1981, 66). He has in mind a "certain minimum level of physical health and the acquisition of basic skills like reading and writing." Suppose that we think of the skills signified by a high school diploma as minimally adequate for living a fulfilling life in a complex, modern society. If we were to adopt this standard for a minimum end, then in primary and secondary school classrooms students who were well endowed for academics should, according to Rawls' principle, help slower students complete the assignments after they finished the assignments themselves. According to this democratic egalitarian theory, it is not permissible for the better endowed to go beyond a minimum level of achievement until everyone in the class has been helped to reach the minimum level.

It could be said in defense of Rawls' theory that guaranteeing access for the less talented to the talents of the better endowed might reduce the discouragement that sometimes comes from observing one's inferiority to others. Recall that in Chapter 2 I brought out the fact that liberal egalitarian teachers have a duty to motivate students to overcome negative attitudes aroused by unfavorable social comparisons. I maintained that one of the difficulties in practicing liberal egalitarian fairness is that those who succeed at getting the best work out of students of varied ability become duty-bound to help the students overcome any demoralization resulting from comparisons of their work. If students were to adopt a Rawlsian way of looking at things, they might understand that schoolwork does not reflect the talent of individual persons because talents do not belong to individual persons. They might then conclude that there is no reason to be demoralized by schoolwork because the work truly does not belong to them as individual persons.

The Philosophy Behind Rawls' Principle of Collective Ownership

Rawls begins his argument that endowments are collectively owned by observing that people do not deserve the endowments they have physically: "Since inequalities of birth and natural endowment are undeserved, their inequalities are somehow to be compensated for" (Rawls, 1973, 100). Surely the view that endowments are undeserved is correct. People become deserving of something on the basis of what they do (Feinberg, 1970, 56–58).

Because people already have their physical endowments at the time of their birth, there is nothing for them to do in order that they may come to deserve those endowments. Rawls believes that the fact that endowments cannot individually be deserved leaves open the possibility that they are owned by everyone together.

Rawls employs the "expository device" of a "social contract" to give philosophical support to his view that justice is the first principle of public life (Rawls, 1973, 21). This device represents the principle of justice as the outcome of a rational choice made by persons in an initial situation where they each pursue their own good without having any duties to others (Rawls, 1973, 13). Rawls calls this initial situation the "original position," and he characterizes it in such a way that the agents who choose the principle are operating behind a "veil of ignorance." The veil restricts their sight in two ways. First, they are veiled from each other, making it impossible for them to be interested in their neighbors because they do not see that the neighbors are there (Rawls, 1973, 19). This limitation does not necessarily mean that they are selfish persons, but it does guarantee that the principle of justice they chose does not presuppose widespread generosity. Rawls is anxious that justice neither forbid nor presuppose generosity. He believes that justice is weakened if it presupposes generosity because generosity is not universal in persons, yet justice must be universally binding.

The other limitation imposed by the "veil of ignorance" is that persons in the initial situation are not able to know their own physical and social characteristics (Rawls, 1973, 137). They know that they have characteristics, but they do not know precisely what those characteristics are. This ignorance makes it impossible for them to choose a principle of justice that prescribes preferential treatments for persons who happen to have the same characteristics they have. The ignorance is one way Rawls makes the principle of justice chosen by veiled persons reflect the intuition that under justice all persons are equal (Rawls, 1973, 19).

Despite the fact that they are veiled from each other and from their personal attributes, inhabitants of the original position are interested in the primary goods they will achieve under the principle of justice they are choosing. These primary goods consist of "rights and liberties, powers and opportunities, income and wealth" and "self-respect" (Rawls, 1973, 62). Even though they do not know themselves empirically, persons in the original position are agents: As agents they can choose; they can make broad plans for their lives; and they can derive satisfaction from fulfilling their plans.

Rawls reasons that veiled occupants of the original position would conclude that they should choose a principle that both protects their individual liberty and provides for compensatory exchanges between the most and the least well off.

> *First*: each person is to have an equal right to the most extensive basic liberty compatible with a similar liberty for others.
> *Second*: social and economic inequalities are to be arranged so that they are both (a) reasonably expected to be to everyone's advantage, and (b) attached to positions and offices open to all. (Rawls, 1973, 60)

These are the two principles of justice that Rawls believes to be absolutely basic for all public life. The principles are chosen by persons in the original position, who reason that because they do not know their individual characteristics, they each should have, under justice, as much basic liberty as is compatible with the liberty of others and should each accept as well the duty that the better off are obligated to assist the worse off. Rawls' persons in the original position are conservative in the sense that they prepare for the possibility that they will learn upon removal of their veil that they are among the worse off. They choose not to permit their individual fortune to depend upon a principle of justice that does not give the better off any responsibility to the worse off because they may themselves turn out to be among the latter.

The idea that inequalities in wealth and power should be arranged so that they help rather than further hurt the worse off is Rawls' "difference principle." According to the principle, differences in power and wealth between persons are acceptable so long as the worse off fare better with them than they would without them. Rawls believes that treating individual talents as if they are the ingredients of a common talent pool is required by the "difference principle."

The difference principle represents, in effect, an agreement to regard the distribution of natural talents as a common asset and to share in the benefits of this distribution whatever it turns out to be. (Rawls, 1973, 101)

The two principles are equivalent, as I have remarked, to an understanding to regard the distribution of natural abilities as a collective asset so that the more fortunate are to benefit only in ways that help those who have lost out. (179)

For Rawls, the idea that endowments are collectively held expresses the deontological liberal ideal that all persons are protected as moral subjects and that, in light of this protection, they have a basic right to be treated as "ends." When people are treated as "ends," their autonomy is respected by others, leaving them free to implement the life plans that they have chosen for themselves.

By arranging inequalities for reciprocal advantage and by abstaining from the exploitation of the contingencies of natural and social circumstance within a framework of equal liberty, persons express their respect for one another in the very constitution of their society. . . . Another way of putting this is to say that the principles of justice manifest in the basic structure of society men's desire to treat one another not as means only but as ends in themselves. (Rawls, 1973, 179)

The means–ends distinction that Rawls invokes in the above passage was used by Immanuel Kant much earlier to argue that people are duty-bound to treat each other in ways that respect personal autonomy. Thus, Rawls supports Kant's ideal that a moral community is a community of persons who are all duty-bound to permit one another to live their own lives as free, self-determining agents. Rawls maintains that his two principles of justice are faithful to Kant's idea that the autonomy of moral subjects is absolutely basic and should be morally protected: "The two principles of justice give a stronger and more characteristic interpretation to Kant's idea [than does the interpretation provided by the principles of utility]. They rule out even the tendency to regard men as means to one another's welfare" (Rawls, 1973, 183).

Problems with Rawls' Theory
of Collectively Owned Talents

The political philosopher Robert Nozick complains that Rawls' notion of collectively owned talents, ironically, subjects one person to being used as a mere means by another in a way that should be prohibited in Rawls' "equal liberty" community (Nozick, 1974, 229). If it is true that Julie has a general duty to help those who are less talented than she, then is it not also true that when those who need help ask Julie to make good on her general duty, they are asking Julie to lend herself as a means to their own ends? And would not this duty deny Julie the protected autonomy she must have as an "end"? Nozick worries:

> People will differ in how they view regarding natural talents as a common asset. Some will complain, echoing Rawls against utilitarianism, that this "does not take seriously the distinction between persons"; and they will wonder whether any reconstruction of Kant that treats people's abilities and talents as resources for others can be adequate. "The two principles of justice . . . rule out even the tendency to regard men as means to one another's welfare." Only if one presses *very* hard on the distinction between men and their talents, assets, abilities and special traits. (Nozick, 1974, 228)

Nozick contends that people's protected autonomy is lost if they have no right of first use of the talents they carry physically. If the endowments that we carry do not belong to us, then it would appear to be impossible for us to live our own lives.

Rawls could answer Nozick's criticism by arguing that the morally protected autonomy of individuals is not compromised by the principle of collectively owned talents because the talents are not constituents of the protected individuals (Sandel, 1982, 85). Rawls could maintain that persons are protected individuals *with* endowments but they are not protected *because* they have the endowments. Rawls' conception divides a person into two distinct parts. One part, the agent, makes plans and moral choices, while the other, the physical person, acts upon them. Because there is no normative connection between the person as agent and the person as physical being, collective ownership of physical talents cannot have any bearing on the freedom of the person as agent. Thus, Rawls could respond to Nozick that when Pam and the other classmates make demands upon the talent for math that Julie has physically, they are not in fact restricting the freedom of Julie as a moral agent because there is no linkage between the agent and the carrier of talents.

If Rawls were to confront Nozick with the above argument, Rawls would be denying that there is a possessive relationship between persons as moral agents and the endowments they bear as physical beings. Yet without that possessive relationship, agents would not be free to live their own lives in the physical world. Michael Sandel brings out the problem very well.

> The notion that only my assets are being used as a means, not me [as a moral agent], threatens to undermine the plausibility, even the coherence, of the very distinction it invokes. It suggests that on the difference principle, we can take seriously the distinction between persons only by taking metaphysically the distinction between a person and his attributes. But this has the consequence of leaving us with a subject so shorn of empirically-identifiable characteristics (so "purified," in Nozick's word), as to resemble after all the Kantian transcendent or disembodied subject Rawls set out to avoid. It would seem that Rawls escapes the charge of inconsistency only at the principle of incoherence, and that Nozick's objection to the difference principle therefore succeeds. (Sandel, 1982, 79)

Sandel is correct. Rawls sacrifices the coherence of his conception of a person by exaggerating his distinction between persons as moral agents and persons as the carriers of physical characteristics. His position makes it impossible for us to have a conception of moral agents who are situated in the physical world and who go about pursuing their plans in the world. The position is not acceptable because the freedom of moral agents is trivialized if it is a freedom that cannot be affected by anything happening in the world. Rawls has "purified" freedom so much that it is no longer of any earthly importance.

Unlike Rawls, liberal egalitarians are free to speak of individual moral agents living in the physical world, because they conceive of the agents as being normatively connected to the endowments carried by them. As we have said before, liberal egalitarians hold that endowments belong to the individuals to whom they are physically connected. On the basis of the right of first use provided by that normative relationship, individuals are equipped to implement their plans. Liberal egalitarians can concede to Rawls that people do not deserve the endowments they have had since birth, without also having to concede that the endowments should not be thought of as belonging to individuals. "Not deserving the endowments, the endowments do not belong to individuals": This is Rawls' reasoning. A liberal egalitarian reply to Rawls would be: "Although they do not deserve endowments, people are nevertheless *entitled* to the endowments they bear physically, because without privileged access to the endowments they cannot act freely in the world."

The Utilitarian Motive

One of the possible motives Julie could have for helping Pam learn the Spanish vocabulary is to contribute to the amount of academic achievement in her classroom. If we think of academic achievement as a good, then Julie is harboring a "utilitarian" motive (according to utilitarian ethics, morality consists of minimizing evil and maximizing good). More exactly, there are two kinds of utilitarians, act and rule. Act utilitarians hold that an action is right if and only if it produces more good than would be produced by any other action performed in its place. On the other hand, rule utilitarians take the view that an action is right if and only if it obeys a rule that would, if obeyed by everyone, produce more good than could be produced by a contrary rule. The practical difference between the two versions of utilitarianism may not be apparent. Think, for example, of the duty to keep promises. An act utilitarian would accept the breaking of a promise if there were reason to expect that doing so would, in that particular situation, lead to more good than would be produced by keeping the promise. On the other hand, a rule utilitarian might reason that the promise should be kept because generally promise keeping produces more good than would be produced otherwise. Both kinds of utilitarians determine what ought to be done on the basis of what is needed for good, but they differ with respect to the way people should make their utility estimations.

Let us suppose, for the sake of simplicity and precision, that Julie's utilitarian motive is of the act variety (my criticism of the motive would remain the same if it were of the rule variety). Julie reasons that at that time on that particular day she can produce more good by helping Pam than she could produce in any other way. For an adolescent to have such a motive is not as implausible as it might appear at first glance. Perhaps Julie thinks of her Spanish class as in competition with another class, and she wants "her" class to perform better on the upcoming test than the competition. Or, Julie may believe that her country will be better off to the degree that citizens know Spanish, because Hispanic immigration is transforming the country into a multilingual society. Whatever her reasoning, Julie's utilitarian motive is not so much to help Pam as a person as it is to contribute, by helping Pam, to the degree of fluency within her class. Julie reasons that by helping Pam raise her score, she will have helped the overall class average.

To see what would be wrong with Julie's motive to raise the class average by helping Pam, imagine that some severely handicapped students have been mainstreamed into Julie's and Pam's class. These handicapped students learn Spanish with great difficulty and sometimes quickly forget what they have learned. A utilitarian might reason that students like Julie who are good at Spanish should concentrate on the handicapped in order to do all they can to increase the academic achievement in the class. However, in every class there is a limited amount of time to help people. For the utilitarian the issue really is, "in a limited amount of time, how can I most effectively help people in order to maximize the good?" Putting a large proportion of the time into helping those who learn slowly might not be the best strategy. It might be better to concentrate on those who learn quickly and who therefore will achieve the greatest gains in the least amount of time. The utilitarian principle would condone this. The principle concentrates on the *amount of good*, not on the *individual* persons who receive the good. Thus, if the good can be increased by concentrating on some persons at the expense of others, that concentration is morally warranted, the utilitarian would say. The issue is not who needs help the most because they are furthest behind, but who can accomplish the most when provided with help, which is limited because of the time constraint.

Liberal egalitarians complain that utilitarian motives violate the equality of individual persons by valuing the maximization of the overall good more highly than a fair distribution of goods among persons. Fairness is the overriding liberal egalitarian principle: It would not be right, as Jim McGraw remarked, to "write students off" because they are all equally entitled to attention, even if they learn slowly. Students are not treated as equals when a talented student like Julie systematically ignores the handicapped because it is less efficient to help the handicapped. Admittedly, Julie cannot help everyone at once; nevertheless, she should not suggest that the handicapped are less than full-fledged members of the class by "writing them off."

In summary, Rawls' general duty theory protects handicapped students from being written off by their teacher or classmates, but it also denies to individuals the endowments they must have if they are to live their own lives in the physical world. On the other hand, the motive to help someone in order to increase as much as possible the amount of good in the world implies that people are not equal. Rawls' theory leaves individuals unequipped to live their own lives in the world; utilitarian theory endorses motives that emphasize good at the expense of equality. Therefore, liberal egalitarians must look elsewhere for their ideal motive for collaboration among students on academic work.

The Motive to Fulfill a Specific Duty to Someone

In the third example, Julie helps Pam because Pam helped Julie earlier with a chemistry assignment. Julie and Pam imposed upon themselves a specific duty to each other and no one else. Unlike the general duties that apply to everyone unconditionally, specific duties come into being when individual persons choose to assume some obligation toward each other. Thus, a specific duty to apply one's own endowments to helping someone else does not deny, in the way that Rawls' "difference principle" does, individuals the freedom to live their own lives in the physical world. In the course of living their own lives and pursuing their own plans, individuals may freely impose specific duties upon themselves. These specific duties bind them, but the binding does not deny them freedom because they exercised their freedom to impose the duties. Accordingly, Julie and Pam are bound by a pledge that they freely made to each other. The specific duty they have to each other will be ended as soon as Julie finishes reviewing the vocabulary with Pam.

Julie's motive to fulfill her duty to Pam is not the ideal motive for collaborating, even though it does not imply that Julie has no right to the freedom she must have to live her own life. The reason it is not ideal is that it implies that it is permissible to favor some persons over others, and this implication is not compatible with the liberal egalitarian claim that morally all people are equal. People are not equally endowed; unfortunately, some are so poorly endowed in so many areas that they seldom have any valuable service to exchange for help they receive. Julie is collaborating with Pam in their Spanish class because Pam was qualified to help Julie with chemistry. But what about the students who are poor in just about all of their classes? These poor students have no academic strengths that could attract their classmates into alliances bound by an exchange of promises to collaborate.

Generosity as a Motive

In helping Pam in order to fulfill a specific duty, Julie is prompted not by Pam's well-being, but by her own well-being. Julie is helping Pam because this is one way she, Julie, can get the help she needs with the chemistry assignment. We are witnessing in this instance two people exchanging services because they each want to do their own best work. They are not being benevolent toward each other as much as they are being resourceful in getting the help they need for their own good.

Sometimes, however, people impose a specific duty upon themselves simply for the sake of helping others, not to get something in return. Imagine that a civic-minded neighbor of yours pledges to donate a certain sum to the local library each year for the next five years. The pledge is to be recorded as an anonymous gift. This neighbor is not favoring herself in the way that Julie's desire to get some good for herself led her to enter into the alliance with Pam. The neighbor simply wants to help other library users in the community, and the duty she is freely imposing upon herself is the way she will fulfill her ambition. She will be pleased to the extent that she succeeds in helping others in the community. The neighbor's motive is basically to be generous to others, much like Julie's motive in the fourth example is to be generous to Pam by helping her learn the vocabulary. Julie is interested in making Pam's life better for Pam.

When people pay a clerk for the groceries they have placed in their shopping cart, they are not being generous; instead, they are fulfilling a debt they have to the store for the groceries they are taking home (Hunt, 1975, 236). When Julie's mother, the philosophy professor, grades papers, she is not being generous either. She is giving the papers the grades they deserve. Generosity is not a matter of fulfilling a debt, of giving persons what they deserve, or of being fair to persons. People are generous when they are moved to do good to others simply because they regard it as good to do good. When people are being generous, they disregard what is owed to persons according to the principle of fairness.

People who are being generous simply regard their activity "under some aspect of the good": They simply are doing good to others because they want to do good (Hunt, 1975, 239). Some people are described as being naturally generous: This means that they could not be other than generous, just as people who have perfect pitch could not do otherwise than recognize a note when they hear it. Naturally generous people do not choose to be generous; they simply are being the only kind of person they can be. Nevertheless, people who are not especially generous by nature can be generous because they choose to be. They can exercise their freedom by doing good to others simply because they regard it as good to do good.

Whether or not an act is generous is determined by the motive of the agent of the act, not by the degree to which the act measures up to some objective standard. Thus an act could be both generous (because the agent simply wants to do good for the sake of doing good) and imprudent or unfair (because the act does not satisfy the objective standard of prudence or fairness). I recall that when I was a child my relatives often generously gave me clothing that was not the right style for me or that did not fit. The givers were being both generous and imprudent (Hunt, 1975, 239).

The Possibility of Students Generously Playing to Win

Motivated to do good to someone for the sake of goodness, generous persons sometimes actually do harm. Suppose two parents give their son a skate board, which he has been wanting for months. The son goes out and breaks his leg trying to master the board. The parents gave the gift in a generous spirit, but they find that they made a mistake because it turns out that the son is not yet coordinated enough to handle a skate board. Sometimes generosity actually reduces the freedom of the person who is the object of the generosity. Suppose a couple arranges to pay all the college expenses that will be incurred by their daughter, but only for a college that they approve of. They want to help their daughter, yet their way of providing the help limits her freedom. Some expressions of generosity are not praiseworthy.

The more that is known about what people's interests really are, the more likely it is that the generosity extended to them will be prudent. Robert Slavin's academic games have the advantage of limiting by their rules what students can do to help each other. For example, if Jim Hall were to use the STAD game in his Spanish class, Julie and Pam would have to concentrate on Spanish vocabulary in order to play the game. The game would make it unnecessary for the girls to decide what they should do in order to help each other, because the only way to play the game is by learning the vocabulary words. The game makes it less likely that students will, because of misguided generosity, provide unneeded help or violate each other's freedom.

Would the incentive to be on the victorious STAD team make Pam and Julie so preoccupied with victory that they would not help each other simply for the sake of doing good? Perhaps it would, but not necessarily. I can remember being helped when I was a high school student by some of my teammates to improve upon a skill, and I knew that they were helping me in order to make victory more likely for themselves, not because they cared about my good. But I knew that other teammates were different; they helped me because they wanted to increase my satisfaction from playing my position well, and they thought that satisfaction was good in itself. Julie and Pam could have such a motive when they play their STAD Spanish game. They could have multiple motives, not just one: They could help each other in order to make victory for themselves and their teammates more likely, and they could help in order to do each other some good. People need not, and often do not, harbor their motives one at a time.

Researchers might find that Slavin's games in fact do little to encourage students to help each other in a generous spirit. Nevertheless, the games could be worthwhile because they are one way teachers can involve somewhat selfish students in academically relevant forms of collaboration. The experience of collaborating at academic games, if only for the rather narrow goal of a team victory, might serve as a basis for later becoming generously oriented toward classmates. For selfish students to develop into students who care about the welfare of others, they must first be inspired to act in ways consistent with generosity, even though they are not yet actually generous. Slavin's games are one way teachers can provide that inspiration.

The philosopher Paul Taylor maintains that education is nonobligatory virtues like amiability and generosity involves (1) habituating persons to actions that are consistent with the virtues, (2) placing persons in situations where moral feelings and attitudes are appropriate, (3) challenging persons to imagine what it would be like to be the one who is being affected by their actions, and (4) helping persons become as clear and consistent as possible about the principles behind the virtues (Taylor, 1964–1965, 27). Teachers could use Slavin's games to take at least three of Taylor's four steps toward the development of virtues. The games would put students in situations where "moral feelings" are appropriate, although not necessary; they would contribute to the habit of collaborating with others; and they would challenge students to imagine the results of the assistance they give, because helpers need to know their results in order to be effective. Taking these steps would be the most any teacher could do to foster generosity among students. No teacher can compel students to be generous toward each other: Virtues cannot be aroused in human beings on command. All that can be done is to involve students in activities that are consistent with the virtues and to hope that the activities will make it possible for the students to acquire the virtues in due course.

Encouraging Collaboration Without Extrinsic Rewards

Research by Shlomo Sharan at Tel-Aviv University confirms that sometimes students willingly collaborate even though they have no extrinsic reward to gain. Sharan has developed what he calls a Group-Investigation (G-I) method for collaborative studying (Sharan, 1984, 4). A classroom of students is divided up into small, mixed-ability groups of students who are all interested in one topic. The small groups plan their investigation of their topic in a way that gives each group member or pair of members a relevant subtopic to work on. After the subtopic research has been completed, the members gather together and report their results to each other. Then, they work as an entire group by pulling the subtopic reports together into a comprehensive group report, which is presented to the entire class. Sharan's comparison of his G-I approach with Slavin's STAD game approach shows that in literature classes the G-I students do better than the STAD students at answering high-level questions (Sharan, 1984, 134). On the other hand, the STAD students do better than the G-I students at answering simple memory questions. Comparing these two groups of collaborating students with students who routinely worked alone on their research assignments, Sharan finds that students who have experience with collaboration are less competitive toward each other than students who have never collaborated. Sharan concludes: "We argue, supported by the data collected in this experiment, that the cooperative social process, not the reward structure of the method's procedures, constitutes the critical element in the cooperative-learning methods that motivates pupils to work for academic goals" (Sharan, 1984, 137). This conclusion suggests that it may be possible to wean students from competitive collaboration to group investigation activities in which the only satisfactions are learning something about a topic and helping fellow researchers.

It would not be easy for a teacher to implement Sharan's approach to collaborative studying in a classroom where students have become habituated to working alone or to competing against each other. Changing habits happens gradually and requires careful planning and implementation by those who want the changes. Some of the problems that Sharan encountered as he introduced his G-I method into his sample schools provide reason for caution and modest expectations. For example, Sharan was fortunate enough to be provided with a team of specially trained consultants who were individually assigned to teachers several weeks before the beginning of a new term. Consultant and teacher worked together by discussing how to introduce the method to students who would be unfamiliar with it and how to solve problems that might ensue. The consultants continued to support their individual teachers throughout the term. Despite the support, some of the teachers tried to drop out of the project even before the term began: They were worried that they did know the new method well enough and therefore might lose control of the instruction (Sharan, 1984, 36). These teachers did not agree to continue with the project until they were told by their principal that it would not be long before collaborative studying would be adopted throughout the school district, and that they were getting a head start with the additional benefit of special support, which would not be as available to the teachers who followed them. That some teachers tried to leave the project is not surprising. Teachers have been told countless times by people who have never encountered the realities of classroom life how to improve their teaching, and frequently they have found that the ideas they were given are simplistic and impractical.[1] I do not believe, however, that it is either foolish or impractical to argue that teachers who have a liberal egalitarian understanding of their work should incorporate some collaborative studying into their classrooms.

To review, my argument is as follows:

1. Development of individual autonomy is a basic goal of liberal egalitarian teaching.

2. Autonomy is based upon differentiations between oneself as an agent and the social features of one's life. These differentiations make it possible to approve or disapprove of the features.
3. Some differentiations require that agents know that all knowledge is based upon partnerships with others who follow the rules behind the knowledge.
4. Knowledge of the social basis of all knowledge is brought about by participation in a hidden curriculum provided by regular collaboration among students.
5. From the liberal egalitarian point of view, generosity is the best motive for student collaborators and should be encouraged in every way possible.

I have argued philosophically that teachers should introduce collaborative learning in order to enhance the autonomy that is the aim of liberal teaching. I maintain that when collaboration becomes part of the hidden curriculum, students gain insight into the social nature of knowledge, insight they must have if they are to be autonomous knowers. As for the practical details of collaborative education, I have pointed out that research by Slavin and others shows that students at all ability levels sometimes learn more by studying collaboratively than they would learn by studying alone or by competing with each other. Collaboration need not involve helping poorer students at the expense of better students.

Reasons Why Generosity
Complies with the Equality Requirement

Generosity complies with liberals' individual freedom requirement because people cannot be coerced into being generous. If they *are* generous, and not just acting in a generous way, their generosity does not result from coercion. Either they are generous because by nature that is the only kind of person they can be, or because they choose to be generous. Some people are generous by nature, but many more are generous because they admire being that type of person.

Can generosity meet the liberal requirement that people be treated as equals? I concluded that utilitarian motives do not meet the requirement. Is this true of generosity as well? Consider, for example, the selectivity behind generous conduct. None of us can be generous to everyone at once. We must identify particular persons and organizations to be the recipients of our generosity: Limited time and resources always prevent us from extending our generosity beyond some point. Wouldn't the selectivity behind instances of generosity imply that the selected are superior to others?

I concede that generosity does not meet the equality requirement when people are generous time after time to the same persons and organizations. That is not to say that specialized generosity is without value; it is more admirable to be generous to some few persons than never to be generous to anyone. Generosity between spouses can be like this, and the world is a better place because of it. But this is not the type of generosity that complies with the equality requirement.

Consider the difference between thinking, "I won't be generous to you because you are not special to me in the way my spouse is special," and thinking, "I can't be generous to you now because I don't have the means to be, but I hope I can be generous to you in the future." People who think the latter way are fundamentally more generous than people who are generous to the same few all the time. To hope to have the resources that will make it possible to be generous to others in the future says a lot about a person. It says, for example, that such people admire being a generous person. If they are not generous by nature, they have made a decision to be as generous as possible as often as possible.[2] Their kind of generosity complies with the equality requirement because it does not in principle rule out any people as potential recipients. The equality requirement does not demand that we be generous to everyone at once, nor that we be generous to persons in the same way all the time. It merely requires that we not look upon some person or group as in principle excluded as potential recipients of our generosity: It requires an openness to others.

How do people achieve a level of generosity that complies with the equality requirement? Earlier I described Professor Gates as an adult who reviewed various careers for herself and then selected a career in higher education, and I emphasized that reflective detachment is needed in order to carry out such a review. Social virtues like amiability and generosity also can be adopted by persons as a result of their review of options. However hard it may be to accomplish, people can decide to work on becoming a certain kind of person. Freely admiring the generosity that they see in others, they too can decide to try to be basically generous. If Julie were to make such a decision, she would look forward to being generous to other students in the future, as she is being generous to Pam now. Even though she can be generous to only a few people at once, she still can devote herself to a way of living that includes generosity toward others as one of its basic elements.

The utilitarian philosopher Jeremy Bentham suggests that civic affairs would be little enhanced by peoples' committing themselves to social virtues as a way of being the kind of ideal characters they want to be. Social virtues are too "disorderly," Bentham says: "There is no marshalling them [the social virtues]; they are susceptible to no arrangement; they are a disorderly body, whose members are frequently in hostility with one another" (Flemming, 1980, 587). Interested in providing for an arrangement the absence of which disturbs Bentham, Immanuel Kant recommends that we see ourselves as having 'imperfect' duties to be virtuous. For example, Kant holds that it is our duty to help others in need; but, Kant says, because this is not a perfect duty that holds in every relevant instance, we are not obliged to help everyone in every instance (Kant, 1785/1959, 41). He explains that we are free to choose from among all the potential recipients of our assistance those in particular whom we will actually help. In sum, Kant sees virtues like generosity as being 'arranged' for civic affairs by general duties to practice them, but exactly when and where they are practiced should be a matter of personal choice.

I am maintaining that the virtue of generosity should be seen as something that people practice because they approve of an idealized character for themselves that has generosity as one of its elements. On the other hand, Kant argues that people are duty-bound to be generous. Now, when I speak of 'approval' the kind of thing that I have in mind is much like the approval people give when, after studying a work of art in a museum, they conclude,

"That's a beautiful painting. It is truly pleasing to look at." People do not have any duty to find some paintings beautiful, but they manage to do so nevertheless. The impression that a painting is beautiful is evoked by the painting itself; it is not supplied by the viewer out of a sense of duty. As opposed to Kant, I am maintaining that the best case for virtuous conduct is the satisfaction that we receive from the contemplation of it. We should not think of virtuous conduct as something people are obliged to do just because some persons are unable to receive any satisfaction from contemplating the virtues. Virtuous conduct would not be as admirable if it were thought of as an obligation. The realm of our duties should not be thought of as so large that virtues of character are included within it.

I have conceded much to duty. As a restrained deontological liberal, I have conceded that the duty to be just or fair is the basis of our living together as citizens, but I wish to restrain the realm of duty to the degree that it not embrace all virtues. That would be duty gone wild, I believe. As I said in Chapter 1, I look upon the individual protections provided by the duty to be just as a safety net for the regulation of human beings when their generosity and friendship fail. I could not admire a community in which people thought only of their obligations and never acted upon their freely adopted regard for others as persons. The generosity I seek, in short, would become "ordered" as a result of people's free choice to make generosity a part of their lives, much as they freely give approval to beauty in art.

The Nonarbitrary Nature of My Recommendation for Collaboration

While I deny that people have a Kantian imperfect duty to be generous, the point of my extended argument is that teachers have a duty to introduce collaboration in their classrooms. If they do not, I argue, they will fail to develop autonomous knowers, which is the aim of the fair teaching that they agree they are morally mandated to provide everyone. In other words, if teachers concede that fairness to students is an essential part of their professional ethics, then compliance with that concession requires that collaborative studying be one of their approaches. While the students have no general, imperfect duty to be generous toward their classmates, their teachers do have a duty to involve them occasionally in collaborations that may arouse generosity within them.

To some readers it may seem that I could have produced a far simpler, more straightforward argument for collaboration by working from a utilitarian starting point. Instead of working from the duty to be just, which is mandated of all of us because there can be no justifiable exceptions to it, I could have worked from the premise that teachers ought to teach in any way that maximizes knowledge. I have not made a utilitarian argument because I believe that most teachers are deontologists at heart. Accordingly, they hold that they have a duty to be fair to everyone, and that their duty overrides utility when utility conflicts with fairness. If my reasoning is sound, collaborative education is not simply an option for teachers who are devoted to practicing liberal fairness: They simply must incorporate collaboration as one of their approaches in order to be competent practitioners of their professional ethics.

CHAPTER 5

Autonomous Persons'
Dependence upon Society

In Chapter 1, I made use of Daniel Bell's observation that a fundamental tenet of classic liberalism is that the individual, not the family, community, or state, is the "basic unit of society" and that in light of this tenet individuals should be free to use "societal arrangements" for their own purposes (Bell, 1972, 40). Some practitioners of the thinking that Bell refers to look upon individuality as something independent of society and regard social roles and institutions as devices that free, independent individuals put to their own private use. Their idea is that people enter into and exit from "societal arrangements" according to goals that they have selected for themselves independently of those arrangements. John Locke held such a view of the relation between persons and society, and in recent times the political philosopher Robert Nozick has employed the view to theorize about the limits of a just state.[1]

In this chapter I shall elaborate more on the way autonomous persons are dependent upon the societal arrangements that stand before them as opportunities for living. I shall explain why Locke, Nozick, and other "classic liberals" make a mistake when they portray society's relationship with individual persons in exclusively instrumental terms. I must provide the explanation in order to address several criticisms that might be made of my argument for collaborative studying. The criticisms would be:

1. that the argument lacks originality
2. that my liberal conception of a person is mistaken about the relationship that persons actually have with society
3. that my emphasis upon individual autonomy is an endorsement of too much individualism in schools and society.

Originality in the Argument for Collaboration

It is true that some educational researchers have acknowledged that the hidden curriculum in classrooms affects the morals of learners. For example, Theodore Sizer writes at length about the importance of making schools "decent" places where admirable values are communicated to students (Sizer, 1984, 121). In one passage Sizer in effect recognizes that students' values are influenced by the way opportunities for interacting with others are organized for them by adults: "How are values taught? Teaching virtues like tolerance and generosity is neither easier nor more difficult than teaching any subtle art, such as literary grace or musical style. It is done, when at all, largely by example, better put, by the 'surround,' by the insistent influence of the institution itself living out those values" (123). Sizer's way of making his point is not exactly the same as my way, but he evidently shares my concern for values that are brought about in students by the way they are permitted to practice living with each other in classrooms. Sizer might agree with me that these practices should be carefully analyzed because they can have a more lasting effect on students' values than that produced by what students are explicitly told about values by teachers and administrators.

The insight that people infer their values from the way they are permitted to live their lives was foreshadowed by Aristotle over 2000 years ago: ". . . in one word, states of character arise out of like activities. This is why the activities we exhibit must be of a certain kind; it is because the states of character correspond to the differences between these" (*Nicomachean Ethics*, 1103b 14–26). I acknowledge that I am not the first to recognize that the process of living among others affects young people's values. Nor are my values unique. Sizer, for example, devotes an entire chapter to the problem of educating American youngsters to have "decent character": "Decency in the American tradition (obviously the creation more of our Judeo-Christian than of our republican tradition) comprises fairness, generosity, and tolerance" (Sizer, 1984, 121). Here, in a single sentence, Sizer endorses two values—fairness and generosity—that I have examined at length. What, then, does Sizer fail to accomplish by his endorsement that I have accomplished?

Sizer's endorsement makes the practice of fairness and generosity in classrooms look simple. Truthfully, it is not simple at all. I have acknowledged that fairness is a matter of duty, whereas generosity is not. Nevertheless, I have shown that a case for generosity in classrooms can be made by dwelling upon the conception of a person that gives meaning to liberal fairness: I have shown that teachers who see themselves as having a duty to be fair to students have reason, because of that duty, to encourage generously motivated collaboration among students. I have acknowledged that as teachers recognize, in the name of fairness, the equality among students and the inequality in their academic achievements, they sometimes are faced with the operational problem of individual students becoming disheartened by observations of the inferiority of their work to that of others; yet the teachers, in behalf of equality, must try to rekindle the disheartened students' morale. When this problem arises, teachers discover that in educational practice the two ideals of human equality and academic excellence conflict. The teachers are not free, however, to resolve the conflict by abandoning either of the ideals because their duty to be fair requires them to respect both ideals. I have acknowledged that when the conflict is permitted to continue, the worst students give up because they conclude that the assignments exceed their talents. Yet, if a teacher lessens the assignments in order to regain the worst students, there is a danger that the best students will stop doing their best because they now find that the assignments no longer require much effort. These are some of the operational problems that occur when teachers seriously devote themselves to the achievement of liberal fairness in classrooms. I shed additional light on the problems and explained that they arise in part from a false self-understanding that is made attractive to students by a steady diet of studying alone.

In particular, I have explained that understanding oneself as an autonomous person is not promoted by a routine of studying alone, because that routine gives students a mistaken interpretation of their work. On the one hand, they can see that their classroom is a social place in which they as individuals are all called upon to achieve the same kind of knowledge; on the other hand, working independently leads them to the false conclusion that knowledge itself is not intrinsically social. In short, because of the hidden curriculum students come to view themselves as working toward a nonsocial goal in a social setting: They come to look upon the condition of knowing something as being exclusively personal and private.

The idea that a person's knowing something does not in principle involve reference to other knowers, when combined with social comparisons among knowers, elicits from students envy and arrogance, which discourage them from continuing to do their best. Students cannot understand the significance of the differences among them, when they do not understand the nature of the knowledge upon which the differences are based. They cannot understand how they each "stand" as an achiever among other achievers, if they do not understand that all achieving is a type of social relationship with others and that they are not alone in their academic successes and failures. Students who understand that academic achievement is made possible by the forms of life practiced within groups have reason to take their accomplishments and failures less personally; they appreciate that if they were living in another society, the accomplishments and failures might be different (Schaar, 1967, 230). Any student's record of attainment reflects the degree to which there is a match between his or her particular endowments and the practices in his or her society. Were either of the matched items different, the resulting record of attainment might be different as well. A routine of studying alone gives students reason to personalize their successes and failures too much, and with excessive personalization come envy and arrogance, which make it more difficult for teachers to sustain everyone's motivation to do their best.

I contend that the operational conflict in classrooms between equality and excellence can be reduced by helping students gain insight into the social nature of academic achievement. Additionally, I contend that, theoretically, a case for encouraging students to collaborate can be made by dwelling upon the conception of a person as a moral subject, according to the liberal principle of fairness. I have shown that the liberal aspiration for a fair education for everyone has sufficient substance to support the injunction that students be directed to collaborate on at least some of their work. My theorizing should give practitioners reassurance that they are not acting out an incoherent morality when they make generosity serve fairness by having students help each other with their work. Instead of violating liberal individualism, student collaboration can further individualism by eliciting the kind of self-understanding that is needed for autonomy.

Liberal Individualism and the Social Nature of Persons

Critics might charge that the liberal conception of a person as a moral subject, which has played such a major role in my argument, is mistaken about the relationship between a person and society. Their concern might be that the basic rights of liberally conceived persons introduce such a large distance between persons as voluntary agents and society that society is relegated to the status of a tool to be used by persons for their personal goals. Put another way, the complaint might be that the individuations between persons, according to liberalism, subordinate the social facts about persons to their identity as voluntary agents, whereas in truth social facts are important for individual identity.

The philosophers Alasdair MacIntyre and Michael Sandel are both critical of liberal individualism and make the criticism of liberal theory alluded to above. They maintain that the liberal conception of a person is implausible because it denies that persons' social and historical circumstances have a substantive bearing on their individual identities as moral subjects. MacIntyre complains that the liberal theory of "modern individualism" treats the "social features of my existence" as "merely contingent" and by doing so it implies that we are each free to choose the kind of person we will be (MacIntyre, 1981, 220). He derisively characterizes liberals as persons who believe that "I may biologically be my father's son; but I cannot be held responsible for what he did unless I choose implicitly or explicitly to assume such responsibility. I may legally be a citizen of a certain country; but I cannot be held responsible for what my country does or has done unless I choose implicitly or explicitly to assume such responsibility" (MacIntyre, 1981, 220). MacIntyre believes, in a way that is not appreciated by liberal theorists, that individual persons are in fact resolutely connected to particular social locations and the responsibilities that go along with those locations.

. . . it is not just that different individuals live in different social circumstances; it is also that we all approach our own circumstances as bearers of a particular social identity. I am someone's son or daughter, someone else's cousin or uncle; I am a citizen of this or that city, a member of this or that guild or profession; I belong to this clan, that tribe, this nation. Hence what is good for me has to be the good for one who inhabits these roles. As such, I inherit from the past of my family, my city, my tribe, my nation, a variety of debts, inheritances, rightful expectations and obligations. These constitute the given of my life, my moral starting point. This is in part what gives my life its own moral particularity. (MacIntyre, 1981, 220)

MacIntyre is disturbed by the way liberal theorists portray autonomous persons as actors who are free to accept or reject social roles. Instead, he says, each of us is bound to some particular role, with its accompanying obligations and privileges. If we think that the differentiations we can make between ourselves as agents and our roles signify that our roles are not constitutive of our personal identities, then we undervalue the contribution that society makes to our identities. Sandel makes a similar point about the distance that liberal theorists see between moral subjects and their social situations. He complains that the distance "disempowers" subjects by stripping away from them facts concerning their situations, making them stand at a distance from society and history. Subjects are consequently rendered "ephemeral and dispossessed"; they are left "too thin to be capable of desert in the ordinary sense" (Sandel, 1982, 178). Sandel maintains that for each of us there are some ". . . loyalties and convictions whose moral force consists partly in the fact that living by them is inseparable from understanding ourselves as the particular persons we are—as a member of this family or community or nation or people, as bearers of this history, as sons and daughters of that revolution, as citizens of this republic" (179).

According to both MacIntyre and Sandel, all persons bear upon themselves certain social and historical inheritances that they should accept as givens, to be forever reflected in their lives. These inheritances, Sandel says, are inseparable from us as individuals and constitute "certain indispensable aspects of our moral experience" (Sandel, 1982, 179). Sandel and MacIntyre complain that liberal theorists disconnect, through individuation, moral subjects from a society and a history that actually give them the identities they have. They say that liberals see society as an instrument to be used by individuals to accomplish personal aims. Liberals, they maintain, therefore do not appreciate the indispensable nature of the social facts that people bear upon themselves throughout their lives, and greatly overestimate the contribution that choice can make to the construction of an individual identity.

The Complaint That Liberal Individualism Undermines the Quality of Life in Schools

The school researcher Gerald Grant has called attention to what he sees as the "increasingly legalistic character of public education," a development that represents for him a "shift of profound dimensions" (Grant, 1981, 141). Grant attributes the legalistic emphasis to public opinion that individual rights of clients should be the overriding consideration among those who provide public services. According to this view, the rights of public school students in particular should be protected by elaborate procedural safeguards. Grant illustrates his generalization that a preoccupation with individual rights drives school affairs by citing the contents of "The Book," a 25-page pamphlet, prepared by a school administration, detailing students' rights, which devotes less than half a page to students' responsibilities.

> In this pamphlet a student learns that there are five different types of suspensions, the least serious being the short-term one for three days or less. Before even that can be meted out, a student has the right to request an informal hearing with the headmaster and his parents and, if dissatisfied, may appeal to the community superintendent. He (or she) has the right to summon student witnesses to each of these hearings and to have an advocate or lawyer appointed to represent him. Before a student can be expelled, he may exhaust all these steps and, addi-

tionally, have a formal hearing with the deputy superintendent and an automatic review and appeal by the superintendent of schools of the city of Boston. (Grant, 1981, 141)

Grant interprets such procedural safeguards as a reflection of a wrongheaded theory of public life. He complains that "public education in urban areas today is increasingly instrumental, technicist, adversarial, and officially value-neutral" (Grant, 1981, 139). A fundamentally different orientation is needed, he says, which will lead students to an understanding of and commitment to "community." He finds in some private schools the communalism and cooperation that he would like to find everywhere.

In the same issue of *Daedalus* in which Grant voices his concerns, the psychologist Jerome Kagan worries about the encouragement of "self-aggrandizement" in schools, which interferes with friendliness and generosity. He believes that other Americans share his desire that teachers promote the idea that "communion" between persons is an important part of life.

> A majority of American families now believe that the balance between self-enhancement and communion has been lost, and the point of tension must be reset in order to restrain complete commitment to self-aggrandizement. Thus I borrow from both the moral absolutists as well as the utilitarians in suggesting the dimensions of character to be celebrated, at least until the balance is restored. Kindness, restraint on aggression, honesty, and a reasonable blend of pride and humility stand at the top of my list for several reasons. First, the community currently needs more citizens to practice these standards, and many youth are dissatisfied with the callous acts of privacy, cheating, lying, and, on rare occasions, destruction of peer's notes they are forced to in order to survive in a system that can award special merit to only a few. (Kagan, 1981, 163)

While Grant blames legalism and its accompanying preoccupation with individual rights for the moral decay in public schools, Kagan laments the emphasis on self-aggrandizement. They agree that the social virtues need to be taught better, but their juxtaposing of individual rights against communalism, and self-aggrandizement against the social virtues implies that they both doubt that a case could be made for the virtues by using rights as a starting point, in the way I have done.

Looking beyond schools to American life in its broadest forms, some cultural analysts have concluded that the American tradition of individualism has kept at bay the insight that community service is important for individual fulfillment. For example, historian Richard Hofstadter claimed that the impulse of "economic individualism" in American history has undermined "fraternity":

> The sanctity of private property, the right of the individual to dispose of and invest it, the value of opportunity, and the natural evolution of self-interest and self-assertion, within broad legal limits, into a beneficient social order have been the staple tenets of the central faith to American political ideologies. ... American traditions also show a strong bias in favor of equalitarian democracy, but it has been a democracy in cupidity rather than a democracy of fraternity. (Hofstadter, 1960, viii)

Long before Hofstadter's time, Alexis de Tocqueville distinguished between a "selfishness" that arises from a "perversity of heart" and an "individualism" that has "deficiencies of mind" as its source.

> Selfishness is a passionate and exaggerated love of self, which leads a man to connect everything with himself and to prefer himself to everything in the world. Individualism is a mature and calm feeling, which disposes each member of the community to sever himself from the mass of his fellows and to draw apart with his family and his friends, so that after he has thus formed a little circle of his own, he willingly leaves society at large to itself. Selfishness originates in blind instinct; individualism proceeds from erroneous judgment more than from depraved feelings; it originates as much in deficiencies of mind as in perversity of heart. (de Tocqueville, 1960, 98)

Even though selfishness and individualism spring from different roots, they both undermine the "virtues of public life," according to de Tocqueville (1960, 98). Both are expressed by caring only about one's own situation; both lull citizens into forgetting their forefathers and conducting their affairs as if future generations have no claim upon them. The lives of other human beings, past, present, and future, cease to be important to those who suffer from either selfishness or individualism, and in the process of seeking their own individual fortunes they withdraw into themselves and miss out on the fulfillment that comes from companionship. De Tocqueville claims that there is much of this particular "perversity of heart" and "deficiencies of mind" built into the way Americans live.

Persons Without Autonomy and Equality

To repeat, Sandel and MacIntyre theorize that there is a permanency in the relationship between persons and their social situations that is not recognized by liberal theorists: They conclude that loyalties to others should be seen as "indispensable" to a person (Sandel's term) and that persons receive from their families and nations a moral "inheritance" of duties and rights that are the "givens" of their lives (MacIntyre's terms). Their theory is that certain social facts concerning a person actually constitute an inherent part of that person's identity as a human being, not just as a performer of certain social roles. According to Sandel and MacIntyre, there is no significant distinction to be drawn between a human performer and the role being performed. They say that certain social facts that appear to be only *about* us actually are *constituents* of our deepest identities; by implication, if these facts were to change because, for example, we changed our roles, we would become entirely different persons.

The peculiarities that occur when people endorse the view that persons are unconditionally bound to certain social facts is brought out nicely by Mark Twain in *Adventures of Huckleberry Finn*. In the middle of one especially dark night on the river, Huck's and Jim's raft is run over by a steamboat. In great confusion, Huck becomes separated from Jim, swims to shore, and stumbles into a household of Grangerfords who take him in, give him a shirt and jeans to wear, and feed him. Several days after his arrival, Huck learns from Buck, a Grangerford boy about his age, that the entire Grangerford family is mobilized in an ongoing feud against the Shepherdson family. Huck has to tell Buck that he has never heard about a "feud" before.

> "Well," says Buck, "a feud is this way. A man has a quarrel with another man, and kills *him*, then that other man's brother kills him; then the other brothers, on both sides, goes for one another; then the *cousins* chip in—and by-and-by everybody's killed off, and there ain't no more feud. But it's kind of slow, and takes a long time."
> "Has this one been going on long, Buck?"
> "Well I should *reckon*! it started thirty year ago, or som'ers along there. There was trouble 'bout something and then a lawsuit to settle it; and the suit went agin one of the men, and so he up and shot the man that won the suit—which he would naturally do, of course. Anybody would."
> "What was the trouble about, Buck?—land?"
> "I reckon maybe—I don't know."
> "Well, who done the shooting?—was it a Grangerford or a Shepherdson?"
> "Laws, how do I know? it was so long ago."
> "Don't anybody know?"
> "Oh, yes, pa knows, I reckon, and some of the other old folks; but they don't know, now, what the row was about in the first place." (Twain, 1958, 92)

Buck brings out a defect in Sandel's and MacIntyre's theory of a person by displaying his understanding of his connection with the feud. He fully agrees that he has "inherited " a duty to fight Shepherdsons because of his birth in the Grangerford family. He looks upon himself as a Grangerford, and to be a Grangerford is to be obligated to be hostile to all Shepherdsons even though the exact origin of the hostility was long ago forgotten. Because Buck agrees that the duty to fight is a constituent of his identity as a human being, he is absolutely unable to disassociate himself, in his imagination, from the feud and to consider whether it is worth continuing. Totally absorbed in his obsession with carrying on the fighting, Buck is unable to render his own judgment of it. In general, when people accept certain loyalties as being absolutely "indispensable" to their identities, they are so permanently attached to their loyalties that they cannot differentiate between themselves as agents and the causes to which they are loyal. Unable to judge whether or not the causes deserve their support, they fall into fanaticism.

Not only is individual autonomy impossible for us if we understand ourselves as permanently bound to social facts in the way that Sandel and MacIntyre theorize, but our equality with one another as human beings is lost as well. Equality is lost because the families of which we are members give us status. When our individual identities are looked upon as being riveted to status, which varies, our identities become unequal as well. Old Colonel Grangerford and his wife head the Grangerford family.

> When him [Colonel Grangerford] and the old lady come down in the morning, all the family got up out of their chairs and give them good-day, and didn't set down again till they had set down. Then Tom and Bob went to the sideboard where the decanters was, and mixed a glass of bitters and handed it to him, and he held it in his hand and waited till Tom's and Bob's was mixed, and then they bowed and said "Our duty to you, sir and madam"; and then they bowed the least bit in the world and said thank you, so they drank, all three, and Bob and Tom poured a spoonful of water on the sugar and the mite of whiskey or apple brandy in the bottom of their tumblers, and gave it to me and Buck, and we drank to the old people too. (Twain, 1958, 90)

As the sons of the Colonel and his wife, Tom and Bob do not regard themselves as equals to their parents. They evidence their inferiority by waiting for their parents to sit before they sit, by toasting the parents first, and by bowing to them. It is not just that they look upon the Colonel and his wife as being the head of a large family in the sense that they occupy superior roles; rather, they revere the parents as being better persons because they see the roles as part of their personal identities. Generally speaking, when people understand themselves as human beings in the same fashion that the Grangerfords do, it becomes impossible for them to see themselves as equals, because they cannot differentiate between themselves as persons and their status.

In summary, the conception of a person set forth by Sandel and MacIntyre is not satisfactory because it makes unintelligible human autonomy and human equality. If we were as tightly bound to our loyalties and other social relationships as they say we are, then we would never be free to judge which relationships deserve our allegiance and which should be abandoned. Nor would we be equal to one another because social status would be a fundamental constituent of who we were.

The Social Dependency of Individuals: A Reply to Sandel and MacIntyre

I have tried throughout this book to defer to the liberal ideals of individual autonomy and equality without implying that society is merely a stage upon which individual persons pursue their private fulfillment. I have tried to bring out the social basis of individual autonomy by calling attention to the fact that it is only to the degree that people are participants in forms of life that transcend them individually, that they achieve knowledge and thereby become different from one another in terms of what they know. My position as a "restrained" deontological liberal should be of interest to communitarian theorists who criticize liberals for portraying society's relationship to individuals in exclusively instrumental terms. I am a liberal, but I have not placed society in a position that makes it instrumentally subordinate to individuals. I believe that I have achieved a middle position between permanently bonding individuals to society in the way that Sandel and MacIntyre do, on the one hand, and rendering society subordinate to individuals in the way that the liberals whom Daniel Bell describes (see Chapter 1) do, on the other hand.

I have stressed that our individual autonomy rests upon a distinctive type of self-understanding that involves differentiating between ourselves as voluntary agents and our social options. Our ability, as autonomous persons, to conceive of alternative ways of living is not something that we have had from birth; it must be acquired. At birth we have only a *capacity* to choose, and transformation of that capacity into an *ability* depends on our exposure to social arrangements that teach us how to distance ourselves, in our imagination from our immediate situations and to look for alternatives. I contend that collaborative studying can serve as one of these social arrangements. The discovery that I hope students will make through their collaborations is that their knowledge reflects "forms of life" that are reflected in the thinking of other persons as well. Thus, for example, the individuality that a student like Julie achieves in terms of what she comes to know depends on forms of life that extend beyond her to other persons. Put another way, Julie's individuality is socially grounded because it depends on the forms of life that it reflects. It would be a mistake to interpret a form of life as a tool for Julie as a person, because her individuality in terms of what she knows depends on that form. As individual knowers, we are dependent on the forms that are reflected in the knowledge we have, and things on which the character of the individuals who use them is dependent cannot be considered tools. More broadly, the rationality of the choices that we as autonomous persons make is provided by rules that no one of us can revise unilaterally. When we take pride in ourselves because of the rational way we as individuals have resolved a problem of choosing between alternatives, in truth we are taking pride in the way we have executed a social act. Autonomous actions are social actions because their rationality is provided by rules of judgment that must be accessible to others as well as to us.

Physical persons provide the volitional ingredients of autonomous actions; however, they are able to do so only after they have differentiated between themselves as agents and their social alternatives. Autonomy involves, first, imaginatively separating oneself from those things that are not oneself and, then, embracing one of them. When young people are inhibited from differentiating between themselves and things that are not themselves, which may happen, for example, because the hidden curriculum gives them the idea that knowledge is, in principle, private, their autonomy is also inhibited. Blinded to the social nature of the alternatives before them, they are not in a position to embrace any of them. Nor are they in a position to appreciate that autonomous persons are dependent on society because without social alternatives there would not be anything for an agent to approve or disapprove of. To have any instance of choice, there must be both an agent—the chooser—and the nonagent objects from which the agent makes his or her selection. In his essays "Atomism" and "What's Wrong with Negative Liberty," Charles Taylor underscores that individual autonomy depends on the social alternatives that provide the conditions for choice.

Autonomous persons should recognize that they depend on the society that is providing them with their alternatives. They should recognize that they could not be autonomous in a nonsocial, state-of-nature situation where there are no ways of living from which they can choose. Simply put, they could not choose their preferred roles if they were in a situation where there were no roles to prefer. If we are to be autonomous, we must live in a society where there are alternative roles to be performed. Moreover, the roles must be available to us: What good is it for me as a female or a member of a minority group that there are alternative roles in my society, if none of them is available to me? Finally, to become autonomous, people must be exposed to social arrangements that teach them that there are alternative views on important issues; people also need to learn how to imaginatively disengage themselves from inherited loyalties, like Buck's loyalty to his family, so that they can determine for themselves which loyalties are worthwhile.

When I speak of social arrangements that help people discover that there are choices to be made, I have in mind not only schools but also such things as a free press, a vigorous publishing industry, art museums, universities, and a political process that encourages universal participation. These arrangements are the mark of a liberal society. People cannot be liberated, or autonomous, without them. Some societies are not liberal. Young people in underdeveloped societies learn to look upon themselves as being permanently bound to tradition, much as Buck looks upon himself. In a way that probably would please Sandel and MacIntyre, they regard themselves as "bearing" certain social "givens" that determine their lives. In contrast, liberal societies provide arrangements that help young people discover that they have choices.

I believe that the lives that individuals choose for themselves receive their meaning from the alternative ways of life that are made available to people by the society in which they live. In this light, the process of living one's life is dependent on the possibilities provided by society. If we are to become possessively connected to the life we are living, that is, if that life is to be our *own* life, then we must be provided with possibilities among which we can find one that we can accept. We cannot volunteer if there is nothing available for us to volunteer for. We cannot choose, if in fact there is nothing before us among which to choose. Furthermore, we cannot choose if we cannot make for ourselves the differentiations that bring into view the alternatives actually before us.

One further point: It makes sense for those of us who value our autonomy to support the society that provides us with the alternatives that make autonomy possible. As a liberal, I do not think it wise to characterize society in a way that pits society against individual persons, implying that individuals become free by liberating themselves from social constraints. I have tried to avoid such a characterization, a characterization that rightly disturbs communitarian theorists. As a person who values his autonomy, I have reason to support the society that provides me with the possibilities on which I depend for my choices. I have reason to support a free press, a book publishing industry, museums, universities, and democratic politics because these institutions provide me with alternatives I must have to continue living my own life. Moreover, I have reason to support other citizens' achievement of autonomy because they will then have an investment in the institutions that make my continued autonomy possible. Living my own life requires me to cooperate with others because I need their help in maintaining the society on which I depend.

I have argued in this book that the fair teaching that is being provided by teachers like the five whom I have quoted aims implicitly at individual autonomy for all students. It is widely recognized that in order for people to live their own lives in our complex, technical society, they must know much. I have dwelt upon the further point that autonomy in our society involves not only knowing much but also having a normative relationship with knowledge that rests upon differentiation and approval. In turn, that differentiation involves acknowledging the intrinsically social nature of knowledge. I have maintained repeatedly that young people today are being blinded to the social nature of knowledge, by the hidden curriculum, and I have argued that collaboration would help make manifest to them that as knowers they engage in a social activity that reflects rules they neither made up unilaterally nor own unilaterally.

I have extended my initial position of "restrained" deontological liberalism into my present position of "restrained" individualism by pointing out the social basis of our lives as autonomous persons. We became autonomous neither by working for our emancipation from society as envisioned by the liberals, who ask us to think of the individual as the basic unit of society, nor by accepting our fusion to social facts in the way recommended by communitarians. The relationship between an individual and society is more complex than that proposed by either the "unrestrained" liberals or their communitarian critics. In their autonomy, individuals imaginatively differentiate between themselves as agents and the alternatives before them, while they continue to depend on society for the alternatives. Autonomous persons should be understood as being neither totally emancipated from society nor totally bound to it; rather, by making use of the opportunities provided to them by society, they are able to live lives of their own.

I agree with the criticisms made by Gerald Grant and Jerome Kagan that public schools today generally are morally undesirable places because of excessive emphasis on individual rights and legal procedures. In Chapter 1, I said that I would not want students to infer from the hidden curriculum that to be a good citizen one must simply stay within one's own morally protected space, which is prescribed by the idea of possession, and never to serve others or join with others. Concerned that students be encouraged to practice in their classrooms the social virtues of friendliness and generosity toward others, I never could be pleased by Grant's and Kagan's findings. I believe that their characterization of the climate in our public schools is accurate, and I look upon such a climate as one reason why students like Deairich Hunter cannot imagine that generosity toward others is an appropriate part of classroom life. The conviction that this is an undesirable outcome of school experience has inspired me to write this book. I do not believe that this is the kind of civic education that promotes general decency among citizens in the public places of our nation.

Nevertheless, I have sought here to provide a moral theory for education that fosters decency, without abandoning the basic principles of deontological liberalism. However much I admire the social virtues, I do not think the best argument for them is made by communitarian theorists. I have shown that liberal theory can be used to make a case for moral education in the social virtues. Generosity toward others is a way of living that autonomous persons are free to choose. They have no general duty to make that choice, but it would be admirable for them to do so. In classrooms, students should be helped to understand the difference between the obligatory and the admirable. Furthermore, they should not learn that the key to academic success is "to live alone in a crowd" and to ignore those who surround them (Jackson, 1968, 16). They can be helped to have their success and to be generous toward their classmates as well.

Concluding Remarks

Some critics of our public schools are saying today that the basic education needs much improvement.[2] I agree. Schools need to do a better job of broadening young people's historical under- standing, of strengthening their powers for aesthetic appreciation, and of enhancing their abilities for symbolic representation and expression. Young people need to learn much more mathematics, science, history, and literature than they are learning currently. I agree with this criticism, but improvement in the basic education of students has not been the topic of this book. My point is that the hidden curriculum needs a lot of attention as well.

If we succeed at upgrading the basic education of students, will we be similarly successful at developing in them an under- standing that their academic achievements implicitly involve a partnership with other citizens? Educators cannot become better at helping students grasp the connection between academic achievement and citizenship until they grasp the connection them- selves. I have tried to throw light on that connection by pointing out the social basis of knowledge. I have argued that knowers are involved in a partnership with other knowers, and that for them to participate freely in the partnership as autonomous agents, they must discover for themselves the social nature of knowledge and approve of knowledge for themselves.

Put more broadly, we need to help students achieve a more decent interpretation of their individuality than the one they are now being encouraged to develop by the hidden curriculum of their classrooms. Students should be helped to recognize that their individuality is socially dependent; they should be helped to discover that persons achieve and maintain their identities as autonomous agents only within liberal societies where institutions inspire people not to remain riveted permanently to one way of life without questioning it.

It is not necessary that we embrace the communitarian conception of a person recommended by Sandel and MacIntyre in order that we may appreciate the social dependency of our individuality. We need not abandon the liberal philosophy that all persons have a right to liberty and self-determination in order that we may justify opposition to instruction that conveys to young people the idea that public places are inhabited by individual right holders who should ignore one another so as not to infringe upon individual possessions. I have shown that liberal principles can be used to support teaching young people, through the hidden curriculum, that individuality can be displayed by collaborating with others and by supporting institutions that help free people from obsessions that make it impossible for them to consider alternative ways of living their lives. Liberal thought is rich enough to support a movement toward a more cooperative way of practicing the role of student in a classroom, but it remains to be seen whether there will be enough public determination to make the movement happen.

Appendix A

Interview Questions

Below are the questions that were addressed to the five teachers during the first interview.

1. How many years have you taught, including the current year?
2. What grade levels have you taught?
3. What grade level are you teaching now?
4. How many students are in your class, or, if you teach several classes, what is the average number of students in them?
5. How broad is the range of abilities in your class or classes?
6. Describe the reputation that you would like to have among your students. How would you like them to view you?
7. On the basis of what you have learned from your experience as a teacher, what do you think basically motivates them to learn? Basically, are they *intrinsically* motivated by, say, the appeal of a subject, or are they *extrinsically* motivated by such things as grades and praise?
8. What are your fundamental goals as a teacher?
9. Now, I am going to ask you to talk about your policies on some specific practices which teachers typically carry out. Let's begin with your policy on the grading of daily and weekly assignments. What are the various factors that you take into consideration as you evaluate assignments?
10. To what extent is your approach to daily grading reflective of your own values, and to what extent—if any—is it reflective of official school policy?
11. Would you elaborate more on the personal values which are influencing your daily grading policy?
12. Now, let's switch the focus to the process of giving students "turns" in class discussions. When you see several students

with their hands up, apparently anxious to answer a question or to contribute information, what are the various things that enter your mind as you decide which of the students to call on?

13. So far as you are aware, are there any similarities between your approach to daily grading and your approach to giving students "turns"? For example, are the two approaches influenced by the same personal values?

14. How about the way you go about dividing up your time among students? Suppose that you are moving among students who are doing seatwork. They are working independently of each other. There are many hands in the air, and you don't have enough time to respond to them all. How do you decide which students to go to?

15. Do you see any similarity between your approach to daily grading, giving "turns," and dividing up your time between students?

16. There is much talk these days about "equal educational opportunity." This is a vague ideal, making it necessary for each of us to interpret what it means. What do you think "equal educational opportunity" means?

17. Do you think of yourself as acting in behalf of "equal educational opportunity" as you work with students? For example, do you see your interpretation of "equal educational opportunity" influencing your approach to daily grading, giving "turns," and dividing up your time among students?

18. Are there any problems with the ideal of "equal educational opportunity" so far as you are concerned? For example, is it not only a vague ideal but also confused or, perhaps, internally contradictory?

APPENDIX B

Invitation to Comment on Use of Teachers' Thinking

In the spring of 1987, five years after I had completed my interviews of the five teachers, I sent them copies of the first four chapters I had written and invited them to comment on my use of their thinking. The exact invitation they received from me was:

YOU ARE INVITED

I invite you to comment on my use in Chapter 2 of your thinking to illustrate some of the main themes in the liberal egalitarian philosophy of education. Especially, I would like to know whether I misinterpret any of the quotations that you provided me. If you find that I misunderstand what you meant in the interviews, now is your chance to correct that misunderstanding. Also, I would like your reaction to the connections that I draw between your thinking about your work and the liberal egalitarian philosophy. Do you agree that the connections are plausible? Even though you may never have heard of "liberal egalitarianism" before now, are you persuaded that you have been committed to a liberal egalitarian interpretation of fairness in teaching?

I have tried to use your thinking in a way that is both correct and insightful, and your answers to the above questions will help me determine how well I have succeeded. After you comment on the correctness and the cogency of my interpretations of your thinking, I would welcome what you have to say on any other aspect of my argument. Address anything that concerns you. For example, how revealing do you find my investigation of the conception of a person as a moral subject, especially my investigation of the contribution made by the idea of possession to the conception? Have I recognized the relevant facts concerning what actually happens in classrooms daily as you proceed with your lessons? Do you agree that the implications of the hidden curriculum for civic education is an important subject for investigation? There are many issues related to the subject of this book, and you are welcome to address any of them of special concern to you.

My reason for asking the teachers to comment on my interpretation of their thinking and my argument for collaboration was twofold. First, I believed that it would not be right for me to incorporate the thinking of persons into a book without giving them the opportunity to correct what they regarded as my mistaken interpretations. Second, I hoped that the teachers would react one way or another to my claim that the hidden curriculum of classrooms is an important subject for investigation.

At the time I extended the invitation to the teachers, I had in mind several plans for the rest of the book; the one I would follow would depend on the number of teachers who accepted the invitation. If all five accepted, my plan was to report their assessments in a fifth chapter, along with my reactions to the assessments. If only a few replied, my plan was to report the assessments in an appendix. I gave the teachers two months to reply, which I later extended to four months. As things turned out, only two were able to find the time to write, and their assessments are reported below. Two others, Verne Vackaro and Jan Heckman, first told me that they would send in comments, but were not able to find the time to do so. The fifth teacher, Jim Hall, told me shortly after he received the invitation that he would not have time to respond. Jim McGraw's and Donna Duffy's replies follow.

Jim McGraw

(*July* 1987)

I. *Reflection on the Liberal Egalitarian Philosophy*
I agree with your stand on the topic of students with natural endowments, and the question of the more immature student with socially conditioned "attributes." Relating my views from the interview is very consistent, I feel, with your philosophy of

teachers acting as liberal egalitarians. My goal, and much of my effort, these past 17 years has been to approach each student individually, and to search out his or her peak level of ability, regardless of social or family background. How very difficult this attitude is to sustain at times! Frustration, parental conflict, and daily fatigue can challenge the best of teachers as they attempt to view the "individual," the potential learner behind the many faces occupying those desks.

You mention the possible restraints on a student, either from home or society at large, which tend to discourage them in reaching their peak of ability. I would caution the new incoming teachers of today that not only will the *students* often be conditioned to self-evaluate their potential far too low, but more often than not, as you allude to within your text, the parents will show support for the same conditioned thinking. Many parent/teacher conferences have shown me the unfortunate situation of a parent echoing the sentiments I have heard from the student within the classroom: "Tom's sister didn't like history either, but we'll be happy with *passing* credit of some kind!"

Although the rate of success with any given group of students is and always will be difficult to predict, I agree with the concept that the professional, serious-minded teacher will strive to ensure that students are given an environment that will allow them to achieve to their maximum ability. Whether that learning goal is successful will of course be determined by a myriad of teacher and student stimuli-and-response situations, the development of a teacher/student friendship and trust, and a teacher/parent relationship to give the efforts support.

II. *Reactions to Interview Material and Connections with the Egalitarian Philosophy*

I was very interested in your use of the interview material within this chapter, and thought I might comment on some areas.

A. On the subject of socially conditioned attitudes and the teacher's efforts to try and "disconnect" those attitudes from the student: I could not help but think of how many hours I and many other teachers have spent in that endeavor. Furthermore, the absence of this attempt, it seems to me, is one of the first symptoms of burnout with today's educators. The strength and desire to pull that student away from those damaging conditioned attitudes is severely tested in any teacher's personal makeup as the years pass by. When that effort dies within the classroom teacher, it is a very sad situation to observe. We have all seen it happen to colleagues, and it threatens us all.

B. On the subject of the moral worth of students and their right to psychological leadership to develop their individual person: I feel encouraged by your discussion in this section that a recent action in our social studies curriculum was, indeed, a correct one. We eliminated department offerings that were strictly labeled "Level 1" for low-ability students. The reasoning, which I think parallels your discussion here, addressed the belief that a student's work should *not* be predictable by his or her social location or by that of previous performance. Indeed, by incorporating lower-ability students in with general-level students, we have seen improvement in the performance of the lower-ability students. Perhaps this change is an example of "psychological leadership," perhaps those kinds needed, indeed *desired*, to have the stereotyping label removed. I would like to feel we have helped them realize an increased moral worth, as you point out within your text.

C. On your (and Jackson's) thoughts about teachers developing a gradual repertoire of approaches—bravo! May every university graduate entering teaching realize the value in sitting down with an experienced teacher and sharing ideas on approaching the immature learner! Indeed, we are pragmatic in our attempts (and failures!), but it is that pragmatism which allows us to adjust to the many different student ability levels that come our way each and every day.

D. On the statement of fairness being the first professional principle among all principles, and the daily paternalism crucial to teachers' competence as fair practitioners: A side comment, David, but I couldn't get this one out of my mind as I read your work: What does this statement say about the teachers, professionals like myself, who *do not* choose to create a fair environment within the classroom? They are there, we all know that. Many *do not* create different skill activities to accommodate the different ability levels. Many *do* accept the socially conditioned attitudes of both parents and students, and they let the "straws" fall where they may—"Take the test, I hope you can pass it, but there's always next semester if you don't!" The question becomes: Are these colleagues less professional? Is it a difference only in style? Or is it a difference in classroom style that is seriously ignoring student potential *now* and that will have its negative outcome on the youngster throughout his or her later life? The possibilities are serious, indeed.

E. On the statement that the "two sides to fairness are not easily reconciled": Oh, my, are you on target with this one! How many times are we as teachers faced with the temptation (or *need?*) to reward that low-ability student with a nice fat 'A' to say "Thanks for your efforts on this paper, I know how hard you are working," even though the paper is far from an excellent paper? The difficulty is the risk that the high-ability student sitting across the aisle may say, "If that's an 'A' paper, I worked too hard on mine. I may as well back off on the effort. I can still write better than he or she can, and I'll still get an 'A'!" I agree with you, we must work constantly in addressing the problem of psychological leadership and the need for classroom evaluation. No one said this career would be an easy one. . . .

F. On the subject of helping students overcome demoralization over their standing within the class: Simply an example of that dilemma: the posting of class point totals on my bulletin board by student number *only*, with names omitted. I think that gesture is attempting to focus that student on his or her performance, not the comparison with the other abilities within the class.

G. On the subject of teachers finding ways to discourage envy among the poorly endowed and arrogance among the well endowed: This indeed is the constant challenge for today's teachers. My 17 years have taught me that I have not reached the level of success in this area I wish I could obtain, but I have seen great rewards in my efforts, and those rewards translate to young people finding more and more that they can shake off unfair restraints on their learning abilities and witness real progress in their efforts.

H. On the subject of students working alone, reflecting the priority society gives to individuals: It is interesting to note that if a teacher decides to create "group work," and allows students to select groups of classmates to work with, invariably the student will select similar students in areas of social standing, ability levels, and so on. The goal of having the students interrelate with stu-

dents of differing abilities is dashed in the process. My observation
has been that some teachers take the time to pre-select the group-
ings, and other teachers forsake the group work and return to the
individual desk work, believing they are helping the student more
with the individualized approach.

Reaction to McGraw's Comments

I take McGraw's "reflections on the liberal egalitarian philosophy" to be an endorsement of my conclusion that his thinking
about his work in 1981–1982 conforms to the basic principles of
liberal fairness. Moreover, McGraw confirms that it is hard for
him to maintain his liberal idealism in the face of such obstacles as
"parental conflict and daily fatigue." He adds that motivating
students is difficult when they and their parents agree that medio-
cre work is good enough.

In Section D of his "reactions to interview material,"
McGraw wonders what I would say about those teachers who "*do
not* choose to create a fair environment within the classroom." I do
not see a choice not to be fair as one that teachers are privileged to
make as a matter of personal "style" or "taste." The choice would
have to be morally justified. I cannot think of any moral justification for not accepting fairness as a basic principle of teaching in a
liberal democracy. I would argue that public school teachers who
deny that they should be fair are wrong.

Donna Duffy

(*August 1987*)

Since I participated in Dr. Bricker's survey in 1982, I have
added French to my list of teaching experiences. What I've added
to my philosophy of teaching since then is amazing. Some of it is
directly related to being an instant French teacher. My double
major of French/English in 1972 seemed like ancient history
when I had been teaching for 12 years and I was told to become
"the French teacher." I was pretty comfortable after all the time in
the English classroom and I was not ready for the shock of being a

beginning teacher again. Very few of my techniques or styles of English teaching seemed to transfer to French.

One major shift was immediately obvious. The demand for me to be involved with the content was constant, and class time for reading and writing was returned to basics. I became very aware of how little content I had worked with in English and how much my teaching had developed into a self-worth orientation.

These basic ideals were much harder to transmit in the language classroom where students were either proficient or not. It suddenly felt very black and white, whereas grades had always been a grey area for me previously. The whole focus of tests and quizzes was especially difficult, considering the extent to which I was teaching writing courses exclusively. So during this time of transition I began to look at just what I had been doing in the classroom until that time, and how my teaching has evolved since then.

Teaching English. What a lofty ideal. Mention that phrase to most people and they panic, wondering what horrible grammatical glitch they committed before they knew an English teacher was present. Odd how Americans seem to have disassociated themselves from their language and respect for it. As long as I can remember I've taken pride in speaking and spelling English well, and I believed I was going to be passing that along to my students. As my interests became more defined, my education became more refined and I ended up with a masters in reading and a specialist in writing. Literature courses appealed to me less and less as I became more concerned with my students as humans and less interested in them as information processors. My dissatisfaction grew as I realized that the process of growing up in high school often interfered with the retention of the very information I was hoping to share. This insight coupled with my own personal interest in writing inspired me to teach only writing courses. (Often the English department albatross due to the amount of paperwork.)

Here I discovered that the topics for communication came from within the students, and we began an intimate process of revealing our inner thoughts to the outer world. No longer was the focus on someone else's words, often mysterious messages from the past. The "book" of my writing classroom was one the teenagers wrote themselves. Their own sense of self-worth caused the volumes to appear, and by the end of a 20-week period, I had been able to reach these students in a way that I could only struggle with or dream about in the literature classroom.

What had happened to my high ideals? They had become more realistic and (I believe) more useful. I was no longer aiming for some area of pure language. That doesn't exist. I was instead engaging in a powerful acknowledgment of my students' worth and ability to handle the language I had seen them resisting. It became clearer all the time that their struggle was not with the subject matter as much as with *themselves*.

And as I ceased the struggle of jamming foreign material into them, allowing them the space to share, I had another realization regarding simplicity. If I could create a classroom atmosphere where it was safe to be, where the only real "rule" is that no one may laugh at anyone else, then the experience of being together could be shared, and thought-provoking learning could open up out of this safety.

That's what my ideal has metamorphosed into. That the purpose of clear English usage is communication and if my classroom can be an example of that from me, then perhaps my students will be encouraged to use the opportunity to communicate themselves, not only with me, but with each other.

This opens up a seldom used recourse that Dr. Bricker discusses and that is the value of each other as a resource. From the French classroom the necessity developed to let the students use each other as partners in learning. It was so obvious there that there was not enough of me to go around, and I soon saw the growth that occurred from this.

When I returned to the English classroom, I had a new respect for students helping each other grow, and I believe that my trust of their abilities allowed them to learn to trust themselves and each other. This action went beyond speaking of trust to demonstrating it, which I see as the essence of Dr. Bricker's discussion.

It seems odd for us to come to the same conclusion so many years later, but my classroom experience parallels his contentions. Students who can communicate effectively with each other, who can plan and complete assignments as partners, and who are willing to assist others, I say, are already the citizens we expect them to be as if by magic after graduation. What loftier ideal can there be than that?

Reactions to Duffy's Comments

I get the impression that when in the spring of 1987 Duffy received my analysis of interviews that she had given me in 1981–1982, her immediate reaction was "what a long time ago those interviews were; so much has happened since then." I can imagine that it is a big adjustment for a person who has been teaching nothing but English for 12 years to take on a French class for the first time. One might feel that she is a curious mixture of novice and seasoned professional.

Apparently, one of Duffy's challenges as she became adjusted to her new assignment was to incorporate into her French teaching the procedure for protecting and nurturing students' self-esteem that she had developed in her composition classes. That was not easy because the composition classes had moved in the direction of increasing amounts of self-reflective writing, a type of writing that could not be part of a beginning French course. A beginning French course, with its well-established curriculum of vocabulary words and translations, seemed to Duffy to be just the kind of course that would lend itself to ranking students as achievers and would thereby threaten self-esteem. Nevertheless, Duffy discovered that some of the innovations that she made in the process of teaching French are applicable to her English classes. For example, she began in the French course to let students help each other with assignments because "there was not enough of me to go around." Later, she took this new approach into her English classes.

Both McGraw and Duffy continue to display, after many years of teaching, a concern for student self-esteem and motivation to learn. When I consider what it must be like to be a high school teacher who faces, perhaps, as many as 120 students each day, McGraw's and Duffy's continuing commitment to students as individual persons evokes my admiration.

Notes

Chapter 1

[1]For a more recent investigation of the way preoccupation with individual rights leads to estrangement between citizens, see Michael Ignatieff, *The Needs of Strangers*, which states: "Rights language offers a rich vernacular for the claims an individual can make on or against the collectivity, but it is relatively impoverished as a means of expressing individuals' needs *for* the collectivity" (New York: Viking, 1984, p. 13).

Chapter 3

[1]R. S. Peters is especially eloquent about education as a process of initiating the young into forms of life that make their membership in the society possible. See R. S. Peters, "Education as Initiation," *Philosophical Analysis and Education*, ed. Reginald Archambault (London: Routledge and Kegan Paul, 1965).

[2]For a review of the research on collaborative learning see James W. Michaels, "Classroom Reward Structures and Academic Performance," *Review of Educational Research* 47.1 (1977): 87–98. Also see Robert Slavin, "Classroom Reward Structure: An Analytical and Practical Review" in the Fall 1977 issue of the same journal.

Chapter 4

[1]Seymour Sarason sheds much light on the different perspectives held by schoolteachers and university professors toward instruction in primary and secondary schools. He uses case studies to show that unfamiliarity with the complexities of life in classrooms leads professors to propose innovations that teachers find to be unworkable in the class-

room. See Seymour Sarason, *The Culture of the School and the Problem of Change*, 2nd ed. (Boston: Allyn and Bacon, 1971), especially Chapters 3 and 4.

[2]Long ago Aristotle brought out that virtuous persons choose to act virtuously because they prefer to be that kind of person. What they do is the result neither of chance nor of compulsion; they fully understand the moral significance, *qua* good, of what they are about.

> . . . if the acts that are in accordance with the virtues have themselves a certain character it does not follow that they are done justly or temperately. The agent also must be in a certain condition when he does them: in the first place he must have knowledge, secondly he must choose the acts, and choose them for their own sakes, and thirdly his action must proceed from a firm and unchangeable character. (Aristotle, *Nicomachean Ethics*, 1105a 28–34)

Chapter 5

[1]For Locke's view of the preeminence of the individual over society and politics, see the chapter, "Of the State of Nature," in his "An Essay Concerning the True Original, Extent and End of Civil Government" in *Social Contract: Essays by Locke, Hume and Rousseau*, ed. Sir Ernest Barker (Oxford: Oxford University Press, 1960). For Nozick on the preeminence of the individual, see Chapter 2, "The State of Nature," in *Anarchy, State, and Utopia* (New York: Basic Books, 1974).

[2]Recent reports on the watered-down nature of high school curricula include: Ernest L. Boyer, *High School: A Report on Secondary Education in America* (New York: Harper & Row, 1983); *A Nation at Risk: The Imperative for Educational Reform* (Washington, DC: National Commission on Excellence in Education, 1983) (Superintendent of Documents, U.S. Government Printing Office distributor); Lynne Cheney, *American Memory: A Report on the Humanities in the Nation's Public Schools* (Washington, DC: National Endowment for the Humanities, 1987).

References

Bell, Daniel. "On Meritocracy and Equality." *The Public Interest* 29 (1972): 29–68.

Bidwell, Charles. "The School as a Formal Organization." *Handbook of Organizations*. Ed. James G. March. Chicago: Rand McNally, 1965.

Boyer, Ernest L. *High School: A Report on Secondary Education in America*. New York: Harper & Row, 1983.

Blau, Peter, and Meyer, Marshall. *Bureaucracy in Modern Society*. 2nd ed. New York: Random House, 1971.

Cheney, Lynne. *American Memory: A Report on the Humanities in the Nation's Public Schools*. Washington, DC: National Endowment for the Humanities, 1987.

Dreeben, Robert. *On What Is Learned in Schools*. Reading, MA: Addison-Wesley, 1968.

Feinberg, Joel. *Doing and Deserving*. Princeton: Princeton University Press, 1970.

Fishkin, James S. *Justice, Equal Opportunity and the Family*. New Haven: Yale University Press, 1983.

Flemming, Arthur. "Reviving the Virtues." *Ethics* 90 (1980): 587–95.

Frankel, Charles. "Equality of Opportunity." *Ethics* 81 (1971): 191–212.

Frankena, William. *Ethics*. 2nd ed. Englewood Cliffs, NJ: Prentice-Hall, 1973.

Goodlad, John I. *A Place Called School: Prospects for the Future*. New York: McGraw-Hill, 1984.

Gordon, C. Wayne. *The Social System of the High School: A Study in the Sociology of Adolescence*. Glencoe, IL: The Free Press, 1957.

Grant, Gerald. "The Character of Education and the Education of Character." *Daedalus* 110 (3) (1981): 135–49.

Gray, John. *Liberalism*. Minneapolis: University of Minnesota Press, 1986.

Hofstadter, Richard. *The American Political Tradition and the Men Who Made It*. New York: Vintage Books, 1960.

Hospers, John. *Human Conduct: Problems of Ethics*. 4th ed. New York: Harcourt Brace Jovanovich, 1982.

Hunt, Lester. "Generosity." *American Philosophical Quarterly* 12 (3) (1975): 235–44.

Hunter, Deairich. "Ducks vs. Hard Rocks." In *The Norton Sampler*. 3rd ed. Ed. Thomas Cooley. (66–68). New York: Norton, 1985.

Ignatieff, Michael. *The Needs of Strangers*. New York: Viking, 1984.

Jackson, Philip. *Life in Classrooms* (19–49). New York: Holt, Rinehart and Winston, 1968.

———. "The Way Teachers Think." In *The Social Context of Learning and Development*. Ed. John C. Glidwell. New York: Gardner Press, 1977.

Kagan, Jerome. "The Moral Function of the School." *Daedalus* 110.3 (1981): 151–67.

Kant, Immanuel. *Foundations of the Metaphysics of Morals*. Trans. Lewis White Beck. Indianapolis: Bobbs-Merrill, 1959.

Kronman, Anthony T. "Talent Pooling. *Nomos XXIII*. Ed. J. Roland Pennock and John W. Chapman. Yearbook of the American Society for Political and Legal Philosophy. New York: New York University Press, 1981.

Locke, John. "An Essay Concerning the True Original, Extent and End of Civil Government." In *Social Contract: Essays by Locke, Hume and Rousseau*. Ed. Sir Ernest Barker. (3–147). London: Oxford University Press, 1960.

Lortie, Dan. *School-Teacher: A Sociological Study*. Chicago: University of Chicago Press, 1975.

MacIntyre, Alasdair. *After Virtue: A Study in Moral Theory*. Notre Dame, IN: University of Notre Dame Press, 1981.

Michaels, James W. "Classroom Reward Structures and Academic Performance." *Review of Educational Research* 47 (1) (1977): 87–98.

A Nation at Risk: The Imperative for Educational Reform. Washington, DC: National Commission on Excellence in Education, 1983.

Nozick, Robert. *Anarchy, State, and Utopia*. New York: Basic Books, 1974.

Parsons, Talcott. "The School Class as a Social System: Some of Its Functions in American Society." In *Socialization and Schools*. (69–90). Reprint Series No. 1, *Harvard Educational Review*. Cambridge, MA: 1968.

Peters, R. S. "Education as Initiation." In *Philosophical Analysis and Education*. Ed. Reginald Archambault. London: Routledge and Kegan Paul, 1965.

Rawls, John. *A Theory of Justice*. London: Oxford University Press, 1973.

Sandel, Michael J. *Liberalism and the Limits of Justice*. Cambridge: Cambridge University Press, 1982.

Sarason, Seymour. *The Culture of the School and the Problem of Change*. 2nd ed. Boston: Allyn and Bacon, 1971.

Schaar, John. "Equality of Opportunity, and Beyond." In *Nomos IX*. Ed. J. Roland Pennock and John W. Chapman. Yearbook of the American Society for Political and Legal Philosophy. New York: Atherton Press, 1967.

Sharan, Shlomo. *Cooperative Learning in the Classroom; Research in Desegregated Schools*. Hillsdale, NJ: Lawrence Erlbaum, 1984.

Sizer, Theodore. *Horace's Compromise: The Dilemma of the American High School*. Boston: Houghton Mifflin, 1984.

Slavin, Robert. "Classroom Reward Structure: An Analytical and Practical Review." *Review of Educational Research* 47.4 (1977): 633–50.

———. *Cooperative Learning*. New York: Longman, 1983.

Taylor, Charles. "Hegel, History and Politics." In *Liberalism and Its Critics*. Ed. Michael J. Sandel. (177–200). New York: New York University Press, 1984.

———. "Atomism." In *Philosophy and Human Sciences: Philosophical Papers 2*. 2 vols. (187–211). London: Cambridge University Press, 1985a.

———. "The Person." In *The Category of the Person: Anthropology, Philosophy and History*. Ed. Michael Carrithers, Steven Collins, and Steven Lukes. (257–282). Cambridge: Cambridge University Press, 1985b.

———. "What's Wrong with Negative Liberty." In *Philosophy and Human Sciences: Philosophical Papers 2*. 2 vols. (211–230). London: Cambridge University Press, 1985c.

Taylor, Paul W. "Moral Virtue and Responsibility for Character." *Analysis* (1964–1965).

de Tocqueville, Alexis. *Democracy in America*. 2 vols. New York: Alfred Knopf, 1960.

Turner, Ralph H. "Sponsored and Contest Mobility and the School System." *American Sociological Review* 25.6 (1960): 855–67.

Twain, Mark. *Adventures of Huckleberry Finn*. Cambridge, MA: Riverside Press, 1958.

Waller, Willard. *The Sociology of Teaching*. New York: John Wiley, n.d.

Wilson, Bryan. "The Teacher's Role—A Sociological Analysis." *The British Journal of Sociology* 13 (1) (1962): 15–32.

Winch, Peter. *The Idea of a Social Science and Its Relation to Philosophy*. London: Routledge and Kegan Paul, 1958.

Index

About the Author

DAVID C. BRICKER is Associate Professor of Philosophy and Chair, Department of Philosophy at Oakland University, Rochester, Michigan. He received his Ph.D. from The Johns Hopkins University in 1969. Dr. Bricker's initial appointment at Oakland was in the School of Education, and it was there that he discovered teachers' interest in the theory and practice of fairness. Currently, he is investigating the relationship between liberal and communitarian themes in Jean-Jacques Rousseau's *Social Contract* as part of his continuing study of the moral foundations of liberal political theory.